Everybody Has a Story
Erasmus 2014
Campus Haderslev

Torbjørn Ydegaard (Ed.)

Everybody Has a Story
Erasmus 2014
Campus Haderslev

Colophon

©Torbjørn Ydegaard, 2014
Everybody Has a Story, Erasmus 2014, Campus Haderslev

Cover:
Publisher: Books on Demand GmbH, Copenhagen, Denmark
Print: Books on Demand GmbH, Norderstedt, Germany

ISBN: 978-87-7145-685-1

www.freedomwritersscandinavia.org
www.bod.dk

Other books in the *Everybody has a Story*-series:
- *Alle har en historie. Esbjerg Karateklub 2014.* Available on www.esbjerg-karateklub.dk

Contributors to the book

Anne-Kathrin Eicher
Carla Esteva Beloso
Charlotte Vercruysse
David McKenzie
Ekaterina Abramova
Enrique Gil Matos
Giulia Rogolino
Iana Posudnevskaia
Jeanette Rogall
Jeroen Demaeght
Joana Bildarratz Garate
Johanna Kröll
Jolien Winckelmans
Kaat Vanden Bossche
Katrin Grether
Kouhei Ozaki
Lubos Azór

Maitane Garbayo
Maria Rainer
Nina Trojer
Noriane Chevalley
Patrik Zilka
Radmila Begalová
Sara Engels
Sem Van Hamme
Sjoerd Vermeire
Sonja Zehntner
Teresa Gómez Donet
Tiana Sagaert
Tineke Herwege
Vera Moroz
Víctor Jose Pérez Jorge
Zhanna Kazeeva

Contents

Everybody Has a Story, Torbjørn Ydegaard	8
Another game together	16
I wonder if trees could see	18
My first summer camps	19
A hard decision	22
Ama	25
The Fantastical Adventure of the Lifelong Dream, the Stolen Passport and the Time Before the Sunset	26
I wonder why the time is running that fast	36
I wonder why the sky is blue	37
The story of one usual girl	38
Night Child	41
The brother I've never had	44
The Snow without You	46
On the floor	48
What I would read if you wrote me	51
European dream	54
My little world	56
A beacon of hope	57
Somebody to lean on	60
Chimeras and delusions	62
I wonder what I'm gonna be	67
Wanderlust	68
Birthday Suit	73
Remorse	74
Part of the world or not I deserve to be happy	78
New house occupation	80
One of those special people	83
Take your Pencil	84
In a men's world	85
My life experiences	88
I wonder how it would be	92
The animal shelter	93
People (1)	95
Tuesday, the 7th of September in 2010	96
An Angel in Exile	100

I See Tears	101
Say goodbye to a person, who is still alive	104
A real goodbye	105
What doesn't kill you makes you stronger	108
Future	113
Wind	114
The Meadow	115
Johnny	118
My story	119
For my Erasmus friends	121
I wonder what you should do	122
People (2)	123
Dear. Truth	125
Be yourself, be different	127
The Box	129
I wonder what I'd be doing now	133
Life poem	135
How I met my boyfriend!	136
I wonder why	139
Life is too short!	140
I wonder how the sun can shine	142
A bit of chocolate cream	144
Inside	146
Tree	149
I wonder how it is to be another person	150
Orion	151
Up in the Air	153
Not only a Dream	156
Students' evaluation remarks on the process of writing this book	157

Torbjørn Ydegaard
Everybody Has a Story

When I some years ago was looking for a film to use in my classes – I teach pedagogy at college-level – I ended up with a movie called Freedom Writers. It showed a lot of scenes illustrating all the didactical problems and decisions a teacher must face every day. And it showed how to encourage, engage, and enlighten at-risk teenagers coming from poor social backgrounds of all kinds. And most of all: the movie was based on a true story, and the teacher in the movie, Erin Gruwell, continued to work with her ideas of teaching and spread them to teachers from kindergarten to university and to school administrators and social workers.

Slowly I worked my way into the movie: I dissected it scene by scene and tried to integrate into my own teaching wherever I found it valuable. And I went 'behind the scene' and explored the web-site of the Freedom Writers Foundation and read the books written by Erin, her students and the Freedom Writer Teachers, that she had taught the methods. This was great inspiration!

In October 2012 I had the opportunity to go to Long Beach and visit Erin and the Foundation. Not even did I meet Erin and was taken by her warmth and openness, her eager to listen to my experiences using her methods transformed to Danish college environment, and her willingness to give from her own doings. I also met several of her students from the days at Wilson High – those students that actually wrote the Freedom Writers Diary, and that were portrait in the movie. It is a wild experience to meet people you 'know', or at least whose stories you know.

In June 2013 I returned to Long Beach. This time to participate in a Freedom Writers Institute to become a Freedom Writer Teacher myself! Again a wild experience! For five days we worked – or rather played, laughed and cried – our way through many of the exercises of the Freedom Writer methodology. Erin was heading all the five days.

We were 24 participants: one from Rwanda, three from Europe (Germany, The Netherlands – and myself coming from Denmark) and the rest from Canada and the US. We were a mix of occupations, all of course related to education. And we were a mix of blacks, whites, First Nation people – and even an half aboriginal now living in Canada. To help her Erin had engaged several experienced Freedom Writer Teachers and about 25 of The Original Freedom Writers. In all workshops we were matched (carefully and deliberately – nothing was done by chance!) with an Original, and so we learned to know many of the persons behind the diary entries and movie-figures.

To me the most emotional experience was a group-session where we discussed Freedom Writer Diary #62. It is a story about a girl being raped in by a family-member. In our group were tree Original Freedom Writer-girls, all with scars from sexual abuse on their soul. One couldn't tell us her story, even after 25 years or so. Another was raped by colleagues on a mission for the Army – and still she was proud of her job as a soldier! The third had a story similar to Diary #62. She had lost confidence in men in such a degree, that she had to live as a childless single – understandable, but to me still a loss of life and love.

Back home I am trying to implement the methods with even bigger eagerness than before. This book is an example on this. It is written by the international students at Campus Haderslev during the month of March and April 2014. The story of this process goes like this:

A new project has started: 35 international students from all over Europe, Russia and Japan will over the next 6 weeks be introduced to the Freedom Writer-methodology and at the same time write and publish their stories.

Day 1. We started out with several exercises. In the first one the students had to write the shortest possible stories they could – one-liners about themselves:

Self-development, energy, freedom – the most important in my life. Believe in yourself! I am the mother of many and at this moment my priority is to raise them so they can reach their potential. If you don't travel, you only see one chapter of the book. Goals are important for your self-fulfillment. I like to get to know different points of view and other cultures. Too many decisions to make. I'm like a tree with knots, past experiences have cut me into my current shape. I like to see the joy in the children's eyes when they are fascinated by something. Past is always running after you but you have to live the present and build the future smiling to chances that life gives you. I like to be cozy inside with a fresh backed cake with my friends or my family and a couple of candles. I am a social person because I am used to share with my brothers. Music keeps me going in life. Life is music. You can't buy happiness but you can play the guitar and this is almost the same! Letter and words are like a mixed soup for me! I am a daisy in the sunshine! I think it is important for me to accept anything.

Then we made a Wall of Dreams where hopes for the future were posted and eventually presented:

I will be more than just another teacher. Our school will be more than just another school. Tomorrow will be more than just another day. Find out what I really want and where to go. Happy life near the ocean (LA-city f.ex.). Be realized as worker, woman, mother, aunt etc.. Go to Antarctica and see penguins. Travel with my backpack in Peru, China, Scotland… To become a good father for my kids. Still want to be a superhero – 'boys will be boys'! I want to travel to Australia and I want to become a professional surfer! In the future I hope to be in a place where I can use my skills and teaching to the heart of those less privileged and give them hope…. I did my best, I like where I am, I like who I am. My future is now. I want to work aboard. I want to start again playing the cello! I want to live in a cozy, white house with the one I love and my two kids. During the day I will be at my tea- and warehouse to welcome everyone with warmth and care. Be with the people I love for as long as I can. See more of the world. My biggest dream is to never stop dreaming. In 10 years I have a big fami-

ly, three kids and a house full of people on holidays. Find inner peace, win the boxing with myself and let the past rest. Discover new places. Feeling confident and not left out. I have a wonderful family with 3 children. I travelled through the whole world. I changed the school system of Austria.

These exercises gave an impression of who they are as personalities. But even though you have a personality and feel yourself unique, you at the same time live a life parallel to many other lives. This was shown in the Line Game, which is one of the methods shown in the film. The students stand on each side of a line, the teacher ask questions, and whenever you can respond positive to the question you step forward to line for a short moment. Some of my questions were:

- You come from a family of skilled workers
- Your parents got divorced before you left secondary school
- Your electricity, gas, or water has been turned off at your home
- You have lived with only your mother or your father
- You have been judged because of your ethnicity, religion or sexual orientation
- You have ever been suspended from school
- You have ever done something you knew was wrong just to impress your friends
- You or someone you know has a learning disability
- You or someone you know is, or has been, homeless
- You have ever felt lonesome
- You or someone you know has tried to commit suicide
- You know (at home) where to get drugs
- You know someone who is in a criminal gang
- You or someone you know has been to juvenile hall or prison
- You have ever heard a gunshot in your neighborhood
- You have lost a friend to gang violence

At last we saw the Freedom Writer movie. I made two stops during the film. First stop was during scene 4 just before the shooting. I asked the students to step into Erin's shoes and define her core problem, the reasons for it and the consequences of it. This made the students really think about the task of teaching. They filled the blackboard with great mind-maps!

Then just before the Line Game scene I asked them how to overcome the problems and what signs to look for in the class to see if the suggested solutions actually would work out. Again they came up with very constructive ideas, often very close to what happens in the film. Then we saw the rest of the movie - and that was it for the first day.

Day 2. We started out with the Getting to know you Bingo. All the one-liners from the first session were written on a hand-out, and they had to figure out who wrote what, and to get signatures from the authors of every one-liner. It was total chaos when everybody was asking everybody, but the stories started to pop up – and they claimed to have nothing to write about!

Then they were ready for the writing process! First they had to rewrite the one-liners into a sentence with an interposed sentence – difficult, but most of them got some kind of text going.

The Wall of Thanks helped them even more to see into themselves. Here are some of their thanks:

Thank you to the lady of pupil support who gave me the life –changing advice in 9th grade! I will give my 'thank you' to one of my friends. Maybe you abandoned me but the time I spent with you was really good and unforgettable. Thank you Mom and Dad (Mama and Papa) for loving me no matter what. Thank you for all you have done for me. For all those advises at 01:00 am and for your support in the good and bad moments. Thank you for always loving me although there were times where I've been horrible to you... I want to say thank you to a friend who said that I must go on and don't give up. Thanks to my mum because she really helped me to take important decisions in my life and guide me into a better future. Lot of loves! Thank you, Dad. We had few times together and I hadn't the possibility to tell you before. You sweet innocent, insecure girl with so many doubts on yourself, thank you for being always there for me – even in times when I don't deserve your caring attention. Thanks to my sister, because she is always with me, in the bad and good moments and I know she never will leave me alone. Thank you for all sister, you are my reason for to be better each day. Thank you Kobe for being there for me in the times I needed you most. You don't know how much it means to me that I can call you my brother! Thank you Nina for being a friend in all situations (also for looking after me, when I'm drunk and so on...). You enrich my life and you make me happy.

Suddenly they are not at all just these young, rich, and beautiful students they pretend to be! They are vulnerable and exposed, too.

Making a Sandwich is always funny and surprising. I will not disclose the secrets of the little role-play, but it involves sandwiches, a bow tie and Lady and the Tramp! The point is to create a framework for the story. The students got, and there stories began to take form.

On day 3 we started out interviewing each other using the Open Head illustration in order to give new insights, by letting 'strangers' ask questions – and by being honest with the answers. I had my Line Game questions on the screen as a help.

The first editing of the stories was done as pair-work were students two-and-two worked on their drafts. The idea was to elaborate the stories, to form them according to the Sandwich-model and eventually to incorporate insights from the interviews.

The last and to many the most challenging of the Wall-exercises was the Wall of Secrets. Some of the answers:

> *I'm sometimes not as happy as I pretend to be. I tried to commit suicide, but at the end I couldn't do it. I'm in love with 2 guys. Sometimes I don't know what is real and what happened only in my imagination. Then things start going the wrong way. There are days when I just want to leave everything behind and take a plane or train to a place where nobody can find me. Start all over again. When I feel really bad I need to feel the inside pain outside – to suffer in a 'physical' way. I feel insecure about myself all the time. I often feel left-out. Few years ago I broke into a house and police almost picked me. They asked me questions but they didn't have any prove. Nobody knows that I really did. I'm probably gay! I'm very insecure. I don't like lesbians. Sometimes I am really jealous of my sister. I love sex very much.*

Day 4. The stories are finished. We decided to keep them anonymous in the book, just putting the country at the head of each story. And we then put all the names of the students in the front of the book.

We then warmed up for a new assignment by watching some of the extra material from the FW-movie: The story behind the story, The Freedom Writer Family, Deleted scenes/Another class-trip and Making a Dream. I read Diary #78, which is a poem, and gave the assignment: Write a poem for a poetry slam. It has to start with the words: "I wonder..." Make graffiti on a flip-over to accompany the poem. Both poem and graffiti will be in the book.

Day 5. The graffiti-posters were finished and photographed. And those who dared read their poems load for class. Poems, posters and stories were put together in a random order in what will become the book. We looked it all through to correct names and countries.

Day 6 – last day of the process: The last corrections were done, the text converted into a pdf-file and skipped to the printing house. The book-cover were finished too, and skipped. And in this way the book was done.

One of the things that Erin stated over and over again during the Institute was: *Everybody has a story – and it's important to tell this story*. This quote is now turned into a book-title – or actually into a series of books like this one in either English or Danish. The book you are now holding in your hands is the second book is this series, and the first in English.

Switzerland
Another game together

What about this one? ", I asked but he just shook his head and said no. So we waited for another one. It was a wonderful day, the sun was shining, and we spent the whole afternoon together. Our parents let us take the bus on our own and we spent the time at a Turkish beach. In the water we played "our" self-invented game: sliding the waves with our air mattress. Oh, how we loved it! It was great! We played it for hours and each of us has had his own role in it. My part was rather unimportant but I suggested sliding on the approaching waves whereas my brother had to decide whether we are going to take this one or not. For me it seemed like we waited a long time for the right one but when the moment came we jumped on the air mattress and floated until we laid there in the sand.

Everyone who could see us saw that we were different. My big brother was much taller than me because he was already a teenager with his 17 years. I was a tiny little girl with long dark brown hair at the age of 10. For me it was just my brother and me. But I knew that we weren't the same.

Soon in my childhood I realized that we had a special relationship which wasn't only caused by the big difference of the age. Seven years were between us. He has always been really interested in lot of things; especially the natural sciences fascinated him. A lot of his spare time he spent outside in the forest to observe the local wildlife. Once he discovered something, he wanted to explore it exactly to know as much as possible about it. This also fits quiet well with his huge interest in mathematics and numbers. For me it wasn't that important. I spent a lot of time playing and being together with my friends. In the years of primary school I didn't like it to be alone. I wanted to decide together with others and that we could help each other. My days were filled with activities which I just wanted to do at the moment. I couldn't focus on one topic for a long time. This was certainly a characteristic of my age. And it brought us sometimes to fights because we weren't on the same point of life. With all our differences and characteristics we had one thing that could connect us all the time. It was the humor and our vivid imagination. We both loved it to invent stories or games and make a lot of jokes. Therefore it was never boring for me when we spent time together. He told me a lot of stories which I loved to listen to. It was great that there was always a new one coming out of nothing and bringing me to a world full of fantasy.

Our backs were warm from the sunshine and the air mattress was floating back into the sea. We burst out in laughing and were sure that this wave was the best one. "Let's take another one" I said and I suddenly stood up to find my way back into the sea. My brother followed me.

The little girl and her older brother were excited and curious about what the next wave would bring.

I wonder if trees could see

I wonder
If trees could see,
would they notice beauty inside of me?

Why is all you've ever learned from love:
to love in sickness and in health,
and never watch the sky above?

If I would still love you in the end
or just pretend?

That you are perfect for my life
After years of strife?

If there would be a God above
Would he show me how to love?

Or did he turn off the light
when you decided to stop the fight.

Would you tell me not to have fear,
if you would still be here?

And go with me around the sea,
To show me how life should be?

Because you've seen a lot,
from your high spot where you always fly.
until and after I will die.

I wonder if life is what it's supposed to be,
when I'm without you and you're without me.

Spain
My first summer camps
(The best decision in my life)

One morning in May, when I was sixteen years old and I was in 4th class of Secondary School all seemed normal and I didn't expect anything special but something was going to change that day.

The Sports class started, and that day I forgot my sports clothes (This was a bad day for that because we were in the final of the course). I was nervous and I sat down watching my classmates running, when my teacher took another boy and told me. My first thought was: "I didn't pass", the second: "Well, maybe he only wants to speak about the activity" and the third… "No, I didn't pass". I was desolated and I was only thinking how I was going to say to my mum.

All of the people in the camp were crying, because the summer camp was finished and the children didn't want to come back home. The summer camp was like I hoped, with a lot of good moments with the children, many laughs with the other camp instructors, and many moments for to keep in my mind. I was so tired but I only thought that I could stay another fifteen days. My first summer camps… It was a really nice experience "I will never forget it" I thought.

It was my first job and my future job in summer during the next five years and that's meant something in spite of I didn't know yet.

Then, the moment of choosing my degree arrived and all the concern about my future came to me. It's really difficult to choose your future when you are 18 years old and your future depends on your decision. I had a lot of doubts and my task for University isn't too high, so I didn't choose behind a lot of degree.

Finally, when I already thought not to study and wait one year for to choose, my mum told me: "Remember all of your good moments in summer with the children, teaching, and playing with them and remember your feelings every year when the summer camps finished and you were so sad and empty for not to be with children each day."

That made me think of my life and what I wanted for me and my future and in that moment I realized it I had had in front my eyes every time:

"The children are my life and I have to become a teacher."

Nowadays I remember when we arrived at my sports teacher office, and he started to speak: "Every year I choose two students of the last course of Secondary School for coming with me to my Summer Camps and to do practice with children, do sports, and learn more about this job. I would like you to come with me this year [...]"

I remember how in that moment I couldn't believe. I was so excited because every year from 9 to 14 years old I was spending fifteen days of my summer in those camps and I LOVED IT!

But in that moment, I didn't know that that day was more important than I thought it...

Belgium
A hard decision

My friend Bo and I were always talking to each other that when we graduate from secondary school we wanted to go on a holiday together. We wanted to go to another country to celebrate the fact that we graduated from school. This was also a drive to keep going and study hard so we could have the perfect holiday. A holiday without stress and after the trip we would be ready to go to college. We couldn't stop talking about the trip that we wanted to make and how much fun it would be. We already started to look in brochures of travel agencies and also on the internet to find the perfect destination. Nothing could stop us from going on that trip together.

When we finally graduated after a hard year of working for school, we were so happy. It was the best feeling ever and we decided that it was time to stop searching for the perfect destination and just go for it and pick one. We wanted to lie in the sun but also see some culture sites, so we found the perfect destination. Greece was it going to be! Lots to see and visit but also the good weather to get a tan and both Bo and me had never been there.

We were so ready to go on this trip; we couldn't wait to start packing. Every day we had to wait, was a day too long. But then on Sunday, in the middle of the night the phone rang. It was only 3 days before I was about to go on my first big holiday without my parents. I was the first one to pick up and on the other end of the phone it was the nurse from the rest home were my grandfather lived. The nurse told me that it wasn't going very good with my grandfather. I woke up my dad and gave him the phone. Because my grandfather was already sick for a long time, I didn't expect it to be that bad. I have never known my grandfather as a healthy man, but he could get through everything. My dad said that everything would be ok, so I went back to sleep.

In the morning my sister and I were home alone and we were just doing some stuff. I was already busy making my suitcase when suddenly my father called us on the phone. He told us that my grandfather was really sick and if we wanted to see him a last time we had to hurry. So my sister and I jumped in the car and drove as fast as we could to the rest home were my grandfather lived. When we arrived, we saw our mother arriving at the same time. We went inside as quickly as we could where we saw my grandfather lying in bed. I had never seen him so sick. Watching somebody you love lying there with so much pain was really hard, especially when your grandmother is crying and you know things aren't going great. Two minutes later my father arrived too. When everybody was in the room, it was like my grandfather knew and we watched him pass away in front of our eyes. This was the worst thing I had ever seen, somebody blowing out his last breath forever. I have never been good at holding my emotions when somebody dies, but I think no-one is. Not when my other grandfather died and definitely not this time when I watched my grandfather die. I ran out of the room and couldn't stop crying for hours.

When it dawned on me that my grandfather really had passed away, I knew that my trip with Bo, that I wanted to go on for more than half a year, wasn't going to go through. So did my whole family and especially my grandmother. Nobody expected that my grandfather would die. It was so sudden that everybody was in a state of shock.

Everybody knew how much my grandfather meant to me and that it would have been better not to watch him die. Also they knew that I was so excited to go on my first trip alone with Bo that they were heartbroken for me. My grandmother came to me and said that I didn't have to stay home for the funeral and if I wanted that I must go on my trip. She said that it was my choice and that my grandfather would have wanted it that way. This was one of the hardest choices I had to make. I didn't want to disappoint Bo and I really wanted to go on this trip but I wanted to go to the funeral as well so I could say goodbye to my grandfather in the proper way.

I didn't know what to do, but I had to tell Bo what happened. She was very understanding and didn't push me to choose, so did my family. First I was going to go on the trip, but my conscience could not handle the fact that I wouldn't go to the funeral. So I decided to go to the funeral instead of the trip. But then my mother came with the Idea of maybe taking a later flight because Bo was going to go alone on the trip if I didn't go with her. We searched the whole internet and went to a lot of travel agencies and at the end we found a flight that would leave on Saturday night.

Finally I had found a solution for my "problem" and I could have both things. I got the chance to say goodbye to my grandfather and be with my family when they buried him. In the evening, after we said goodbye and ate a meal together with the whole family, I left for the airport to go and experience what was left of the trip together with my friend.

The three days that were left, were fantastic and we made the most out of them. My grandmother made a deal with me that I had to have fun on those three days and that I didn't have to feel guilty about going on this trip. She told me that my grandfather would have wanted me to have the best three days of my life, and I did together with Bo.

Ama

I wonder how it would be
To be in the invisible lonely town
Where the silence is the owner
The shadows are white
And the stars are going down.

The happiness is the sadness
The melancholy is the satisfaction
To love is prohibited
And to hate is an obligation.

Although I think everything up and down
You became grey in green
The darkness into color
And the shadows in persons

You understand the things
I don´t say and I don´t do
I have learned seeing your faults
They made the best of you

Ama, mare, mamá, mum,
mor, mutter, matka, haha
Everywhere you would make me to be
The inspiration of my person

England
The Fantastical Adventure of the Lifelong Dream, the Stolen Passport and the Time Before the Sunset

As soon as she started, I got this weird flickering in my eyes. What was she doing? I'd never know anything like it.

Sorry, I should explain.

I was in Peru. More specifically, I was in Cajamarca -la ciudad de la amistad, which means, the city of friendship. Yes, that's how Cajamarca marketed itself, proud to be known as the friendliest city in the country

Actually, I probably need to explain it better that that. If you're going to get the full story, I need to take you back a few years. Let me try again.

At the age of fourteen, I saw a picture of Machu Picchu. Now, if I'm honest, I can't remember if this was a picture in a book, or on the television, or in a magazine or where it was, but I can remember saying, "I have to go there one day." There have been many times when I have seen pictures of exotic places and thought, "I'd like to go there one day," but when I saw this picture, I said, "I have to go." From that time on, every time I saw an article in a publication or a programme on the television about Peru, I would pay close attention and, with the passing of time, I learned that there was more to Peru than Machu Picchu. I started to dream about going there, and I even said that I could die a happy man if I could only visit Machu Picchu.

Fifteen years later, after dreaming of it for fifteen years, I finally plucked up the courage to go to Peru and, after dreaming of it for fifteen years, I finally got to visit Machu Picchu ... and it was amazing. I can remember sitting, looking out over the site whilst having a breakfast of chocolate chip cookies and Inca Kola and thinking that, after dreaming of it for fifteen years (have I mentioned that already?) I had finally reached my goal, realised my dream, achieved my ambition and any other variation of that sentiment. I was very happy. I loved it.

I was in Peru for seven and a half weeks, which I thought would be more than enough time to see everything that I wanted to see. It wasn't. There were lots of places that were on my 'to do' list when I returned to England, so I returned to Peru eighteen months later, so I could see the places that I hadn't reached the first time around. Between my trips, however, I began to change.

The first change might sound rather insignificant, but it felt significant to me - I had my thirtieth birthday. Turning thirty really made me question life, particularly my own life. What had I done? What had I achieved? What was I doing? Other than see Machu Picchu, I hadn't really done anything with my life. For more than half of my first twenty-nine years, I'd dreamt of seeing Machu Picchu, and even said that I'd be able to die a happy man if I could see it, but now that I had seen it, what was left for me to do?

I began to read. I read The Tibetan Book of Living and Dying, I began to read The Holy Bible and I read a book entitled ...isms, which was an introduction to all of the major religions of the world. I was convinced that I was not getting the most out of life, and I was definitely not getting the most out of my own life, but I didn't know how to change things. I even developed my own philosophy on life, which will give you, my dear reader, some insight into what my mind was like:

Life is like a pile of manure. You will spend most of your life struggling to get out of it and occasionally, very occasionally, you'll manage to get your head out of it and take in a breath of fresh air and it will feel glorious, but then you will slide back down into the manure and your struggle will begin all over again.

What a lovely outlook!

So, eighteen months after my initial visit, I attempted to steal another breath of fresh air by returning to Peru, this time for five weeks. Again, I thought that it would be more than enough time to see all of the things that I wanted to see, those places that I hadn't reached last time. Again, it wasn't.

Now, when I was in backpacker mode, I would always accept any invitation to try something 'local'. It was this attitude that led me to accept an invitation to attend a church service in Cajamarca. A young guy on the street was handing out flyers and inviting people to go to his church's evening service, so I went along. He introduced me to his friends and to the pastor and his wife and to too many people to remember. Everybody was very friendly, as you would expect in a place that claimed to be the city of friendship. It was nice.

At the end of the service, a young and stereotypically beautiful Latin American girl approached me and said, in English, "My God wants me to pay for you." God wants her to pay for me? I didn't understand, and this lack of understanding must have been evident on my face.

"Sorry, sorry. My English is not very good." She paused, steadied herself and tried again. "My" - she pointed to her chest - "God" - she pointed upwards - "wants me" - she pointed to her chest again - "to pay" - she put her hands together, as if praying - "for you" - she pointed at me. Aaah, to pray for me. That made more sense.

She took me down to the front of the church and knelt down. I didn't really know what to do, so I just copied what she was doing and knelt down beside her. She raised her hands above her head, so I raised my hands above my head. Then she began to pray, but I did not. Why not? Because, as I told you earlier, as soon as she started, I got this weird flickering in my eyes. I guess that it looked like the rapid eyeball movement that happens when you dream, but I don't know, because I didn't see it. The only way I can describe it is by saying that it was a weird flickering sensation, but it began at the exact same moment that Liceth had started praying.

I have absolutely no idea what she said in her prayer. It was all in Spanish - my Spanish has never been brilliant - but even if she had been speaking in English, I don't think that I would have heard anything that she said. All that I could think about was this weird flickering sensation. What was she doing? I'd never known anything like it.

She stopped. Why had she stopped? Why had my eyes not stopped? And what was happening?

"You can't stop now," I said. "It's not finished yet."

Why had I said that? I didn't know what was happening, yet I'd just said - with great confidence - "It's not finished yet." This was bizarre. What made it more bizarre was the fact that she listened to me and began praying again.

While the prayer continued, I wondered what was happening. Was she healing me? I'd had sight problems for a few years - maybe I'd be healed today? That excited me. Then it scared me. I'd like to have my sight back to normal, but if it was brought back to normal like this, I'd be a bit freaked out.

She stopped. As she was coming to a close, she spoke the only words that I understood: "In the name of the Father, the Son and the Holy Spirit, amen." At the precise moment that she said, "amen," my eyes stopped flickering. I knelt there and kept them closed. I was scared to open them. I was scared to open them in case I'd been healed and I was scared to open them in case I hadn't. Eventually, I realised that I would have to open them, otherwise I wouldn't be able to find my way back to the hotel. I opened them. I wasn't healed. I was relieved. And disappointed.

And so I returned to the hotel. The owner was on the reception desk and I asked him if I could have my passport back as I planned to leave early the next day. Problem.

I had asked the hotel if they had any security facilities that morning as I wanted to leave my passport somewhere safe. This was because I was planning on visiting the Museum of the Royal Tombs of the Lord of Sipan, which involved a lengthy journey on local public (and not very safe for potentially rich tourists) transport. It would probably be a good idea to leave my passport with the hotel's security facilities. Good thinking, David. Very wise.

So, after going out for some food which I never found, going to a church service where I couldn't understand much and experiencing flickery eye syndrome (I thought that I would give it a scientific name - it made me feel intelligent), I now learned that the hotel's security facilities were, literally, one cardboard box in a cleaning supplies cupboard and - SURPRISE! - my passport had been stolen. Now, I don't know about you, but I wouldn't have expected a cardboard box in a cleaning supplies cupboard to be considered a secure location for the storage of a passport. For some reason, though, the (lack of) wisdom of the owner had concluded that the box in the cupboard was more than safe enough for the storage of passports and, presumably, other valuable items, such as gold bullion, diamond rings and top secret government documents. But do you know what the strangest thing about all of this was?

I wasn't bothered. I was completely calm. My passport had been stolen, but I really didn't mind. "Maybe this," I thought, "is why she prayed for me, so I wouldn't be angry."

The next morning, I visited the police station to report my passport as having been stolen. This allowed me to secure the necessary paperwork in order to apply for a replacement passport. This meant, of course, that my plans for my Peruvian adventure had to change somewhat, as I now had to contact the British embassy in Lima and begin the application process for a new passport.

This, dear reader, is where the story begins to get interesting.

This was early in 2007. The internet had been around for quite a long time, but I, not being a fan of computers, had stubbornly refused to have an e-mail address. Staying in touch with the British embassy, however, meant that I now had to get one. With a heavy heart, I created a Yahoo account, therefore forcing me to give up my claim that I was the only backpacker in the world without an e-mail address. This made me feel a little bit sad, but the little bit of sadness was soon replaced by an unexpected curiosity.

I had just opened a Yahoo account. i now had an e-mail address. Should I explore the electronic world even further and try surfing the web? Why not?

Hmm. What should I look for?

Hmm.

Border Harriers! Yes, I would search for my old athletics club. If they had a website, it might prove to be slightly interesting. I searched and ... there it was! I clicked on the link and explored.

"Look at me," I thought to myself. "I'm finally stepping into the twenty-first century ... and only seven years after the rest of the world!" It was a proud moment.

Now, I'll be honest with you: unless you happen to be a current or former member of Border Harriers Athletics Club, the contents of their website won't seem very interesting, but there was one thing on that website that had a significant impact on my life and, therefore, you need to know what it was, so I'll tell you: it was a link to the London 2012 Olympic Games website. Surprised at how interesting surfing the web was proving to be, I clicked on the link with no small amount of excitement.

Ooh, London 2012 - how wonderful! The biggest sporting event in the world was on its way to Britain and ... what was this? I blinked and looked at it again, just to make sure that my unhealed eyes weren't playing tricks on me. They weren't. I clicked on ... 'Volunteer'.

When I was a teenager, I loved athletics. I lived for it. And the greatest thing about athletics was, of course, the Olympic Games. My dream had been to win an Olympic gold medal in the fifteen hundred metres, but there was just one tiny problem - I was rubbish. Volunteering, however, could be my way of participating in the Olympic Games. Okay, so I wouldn't be competing and I wouldn't win any medals, but I would be a part of it and, now that I'd turned thirty and never improved in my ability to run, this was the best chance that I would ever get at being involved in the Olympics. I was definitely very interested in volunteering for London 2012.

I read through all of the details with great enthusiasm until I reached their selection criteria. It said something like, "Places will not be given on a 'first come, first served' basis; there will be a selection process, and part of that selection process will include taking into account any voluntary work experience." "Okay," I thought, "when I get back home, I need to begin volunteering."

And so it was that I began to think about what sort of voluntary work I could do which would help me to secure a position at the London Olympics. When I returned to England, with my new passport in my hand, I got a job in a youth hostel in the Peak District, a national park. The nearest city to our hostel was Sheffield, so I decided to go there in order to make enquiries about volunteering opportunities.

I had decided that I would like to work with adults with learning disabilities. "Why is that, David?" I hear you ask. Well, I'll tell you. I had worked alongside two men with learning disabilities in two of my previous jobs, both of whom worked as pot washers in kitchens, and I always had more patience with these guys than other staff members did. Maybe I'd be good at doing some sort of support work. I'd give it a try. There was a lot at stake here - this could be my ticket to Olympic glory!

My ideal voluntary job, I concluded after much deliberation, would be supporting adults with learning disabilities in some sort of classroom setting. That would be perfect, I thought, but I didn't know how realistic it would be. I found a centre which helps people with learning disabilities, learned that they actively encourage volunteers and discovered that - yes! - they ran a classroom-based life skills course on the day that I was available. Perfect, I thought.

And perfect it turned out to be. I loved doing this work and, after just three or four weeks, I said that I had found what I was meant to be doing with my life - this was why I had been put on the earth! For the first time in my life, I had found something that I enjoyed, something that was worthwhile and something that I was good at ...

and that combination made me feel very, very, very happy. If I could do this for a living, I'd be able to enjoy the rest of my life.

After a few months, a vacancy arose on the course for a Learning Support Assistant, which was what I'd been doing in a voluntary capacity. I could do that job. I'd be good at that. Actually, I was good at that already. I could be good at it and get paid for it. Okay, it would no longer count as voluntary work for my place on the British Olympic team (I admit that I may be guilty of exaggeration, here), but I could find something else to cover that. I applied for the job and began preparing for the interview.

The interview took place on Friday 31st August 2007. I always get nervous in interviews, but I did reasonably well. There were no questions that took me by surprise and there had been no awkward pauses, so I took that as a good sign. And three days later, on Monday 3rd September, at approximately half past two in the afternoon, I received a call telling me that I had got the job and that I could begin the next day.

I was overjoyed. One of my colleagues told me that I didn't walk for the rest of that day, but bounced. I had never been so excited about any job before in my life, but I had finally, for the first time in all my days, secured a job that I actually wanted to do. Life was no longer a pile of manure - it was a forest in springtime, it was early morning birdsong and it was the fattest, creamiest chocolate cake that you've ever had.

When I went to bed that evening (early, because I'd had an early start), I reflected on the events of the day, which led me to reflect on the events of the year, which led me to reflect on the events of my life.

When I had began working at the youth hostel, I had had a plan: work until Christmas, have one last visit to South America and then return to Carlisle and wait to die. That really was my plan. Work for eight months, travel for six and wait (for how many years?) to die. Now, though, everything was different. I had found a job that made me think that my life was not worthless, but valuable. I was, in that job, able to make a difference to the world, to have a positive impact. In the space of just a few months, I had gone from 'waiting to die' to 'making a difference". How had that happened? My mind started racing. Dear reader, prepare to read an exceptionally long sentence.

I got the job because I volunteered, I volunteered because I wanted to be involved in the London Olympics, I wanted to be involved in the London Olympics because I'd looked at their website, I'd started looking at websites because I'd been forced into getting an e-mail address, I got an e-mail address to keep in touch with the British embassy in Peru, I needed to keep in touch with the embassy in order to get a new passport, I needed to get a new passport because my old one had been stolen and my old passport had been stolen on the day that I experienced flickery eye syndrome as a Peruvian girl prayed for me.

Hmm.

There seemed to be some sort of mysterious order to this sequence of events that was, in my view, too big to be mere chance. All of these little things had worked together to get me to this place and ...

My mind started racing again. I thought about all of the different things that I had read over the past eighteen or so months, the different conversations that I'd had with people about life, the universe and everything. And I thought about my new job. If I was going to do this job well, to do it brilliantly, I was going to need a lot of help. I made my decision.

It was around a quarter past nine in the evening. There was still a little sunlight in the air, but not a lot; it would leave soon, go down behind the mountains and declare the end of another day. Dusk could be a particularly beautiful time in that part of the world, and I would often go up the nearest peak after work just to watch the sunset, but today my focus was elsewhere. Before the last of the light faded and invited the night to creep over the sky, there was something that I had to do. I took in a deep breath, then sighed it out. I was ready.

I knelt down beside my bed and closed my eyes. I was now totally oblivious to the world around me, cut off from the rest of humanity. It was just me and my maker.

"Jesus," I said, "I don't really know how to do this, but I want You to come into my life, please."

Immediately - immediately! - i had another bout of flickery eye syndrome and, suddenly, it made sense.

"It wasn't her," I said, "it was You."

I wonder why the time is running that fast

I wonder why the time is running that fast
Why you are living in the past.
The future looks nice without a plan
Just doing what you want.

Forget the people and what they said
Just wake up and go outside.
The future looks nice without a plan
Just doing what you want.

I wonder why we can not go and run
go to the beach and enjoy the sun.
Decide, yes or not, come or stay
be a child and come to play.

I wonder why the sky is blue

I wonder why the sky is blue,
and has to rain on you.

I wonder why the moon shines at night,
that is such a beautiful sight.

I wonder why a penguin is black and white,
he is amazing as the night.

I wonder how a bird can fly,
and how I can wave them all goodbye.

I wonder how we would communicate
if language was elucidate.

I wonder why we see so much,
but can't see a light touch.

I wonder how we listen with our ears,
but can detect some fears.

I wonder why we are so strong,
but not always have the strength to carry on.

Russia
The story of one usual girl

There is a usual girl, like millions, somewhere in Russia. This girl doesn't have anything special: she is quite pretty, but there are many much prettier girls, she is not dull, but there are plenty of people much more intelligent, she draws not bad, but nothing worth any attention. So, this girl is ME.

I was born in a small town in an ordinary family and all my (not very long) life spent there, growing up, attending kindergarten, then school, just like every child.

At school, I was an average student with average progress. Although I always knew that I could be one of the best students and have this perfect certificate, if I put a little more effort, but I didn't want and didn't need it really. I had a lot of friends, had fun and just enjoyed my life, instead of working hard.

After school, I took my exams and got quite high results (one of three best), so I proved to be not just a nice face. Then I was going to enter a university, I didn't aim very high, I decided to stay in my native town and study there (whereas everyone wanted to go to a big city and enter a prestigious university). So I didn't even try, though I had chances. And I was quite satisfied with my choice.

I've been studying there for three years and everything was ok. But one day our group was told that there was a competition for a grant, and the winner is going to study abroad, in Denmark, for free. I decided to take part in it just for fun, I didn't expect to win at all (I had never won anything), but for me who has never been abroad and hadn't even thought of studying there it was a great opportunity. So I wrote the letter of motivation and made the presentation, which was written in quite a simple language. My presentation was the first; I was really worried how it was going to be. I just came and told everything I could. When all the participants were waiting for the results, I doubted if I can win, because there were teachers' favorites who did their presentations with the help of teachers and in a very complicated way. They took part in some scientific projects, and what was about me? So when I heard my name, I just couldn't realize that I'm the winner, I'm the number one! I didn't feel anything. I knew I had to be happy, but there was nothing. It was a real shock! But of course, in some minutes the shock passed and it was one of the happiest moments of my life!

Well, now I'm here far far away from my little town, exploring the world! I could never expect that! Now I know that I have power to get everything I want and I will be prosperous in this life. I strongly believe it!

You can achieve whatever you want, just believe it and take every chance to get your goal!

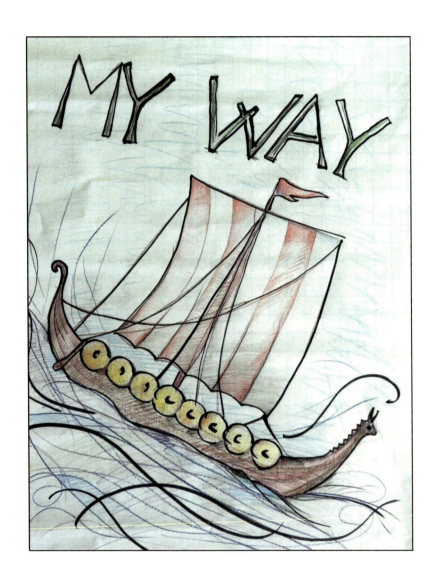

Germany
Night Child

I asked myself, my inner child
to cooperate with me,
I drew things down it really liked,
at night it came to me.

> *Take me by the hand*
> *and then follow me,*
> *I've seen things I don't understand*
> *perhaps you've got the key.*

I got scared about that proposal
thought l knew what it meant,
I didn't want to see it
thought all the pain wasn't planned.

> *Please go in front now*
> *you can help me today.*
> *Why are you shaking?*
> *It is the right way.*

I am as scared as the child now,
dark lights in the end of the floor
I asked her to stop and go back to bed
but she kept coming, coming back.

> *Why do you leave me alone here?*
> *Why wouldn't you come with me?*
> *I thought I can trust you.*
> *Please, please listen to me.*

Thinking about her
tears ran down my cheek
I caused her silence
but hope she will speak!

Spain
The brother that I've never had

My story started when I was born. Before my birth, in my family there were just my father, mother and my elder brother.

Since I was born, my brother started to be jealous of me. Maybe it was normal because I was the new one in the family and I needed more cares in that moment but this jealousness continued.

When I was 1 year old, my parents moved into a new flat. It was bigger than the other and we still live there. Here, in this new flat, my first memories about the relationship between us began. Everything that I can tell from my childhood, is what my parents have told me when I have grown up.

He was always hitting me. One of the worst things was that he pushed me from the third step of our stairs (we live in a duplex) directly to the radiator which was downstairs and I hit with my head.

In other occasion, he launched me a peg-top (peonza in Spanish) into my lips.

We never played together because all the time that he was alone with me he just tried to do bad things. For that reason I can say I've never had a real brother.

During my adolescence, his hatred towards me increased. He continued hitting me and I had lots of bruises until the day that my parents decided to take him to the psychologist. This was a long process. Little by little, his behavior started to change and he stopped hitting me and also my little sister.

He used to have anxiety crisis. I think it was because he couldn't hit me anymore, but I'm not sure because I've never asked my parents about it.

At this point of my life, I was 15 more or less but the story hasn't finished yet.

We tried to have a better relationship, doing some things together. We travelled to ski together several times but nothing changed at the end. He was a nice person during the trip but when we returned back home, the reality was the same, like always. He didn't hit me anymore but now he abused me in a psychological way.

The only thing that I can notice is that since 1 year and a half, he found a job and he spends less time at home. I'm really happy because I can be more relaxed at home and I don't have so many problems as before, but I still have them during the weekends or at holidays.

Sometimes, I'm sad because I've never had a big brother that helps me. Now, I'm here, in Denmark and I can say that the day I will come back home, will be really difficult because he will be there. We haven't talked to each other since I came here.

My wishes for the future years are that one day his behavior changes and he realizes that it will be better to have a good relationship than the "relation" that we have right now. In addition I have to say that I will never forgive him for what he did to me. That's the reason why sometimes I wish bad things for him. It's like the price he has to pay for the damage he caused me. I remember that sometimes I thought about escaping from home or denouncing him to the police but I never did it. Maybe because I think that after all he is my brother, even if I don't like it. It is sad to say that if something bad happened to him I wouldn't feel sorry.

Italy
The Snow without You

It was the 4 March 2005. That day in Genova it was copiously snowing which was totally unexpected. I was 13 years old and I was outside with some of my friends. That day changed my life. My dad, my hero, my young and beautiful man died. While I was outside having fun he was dying from a brain haemorrhage at 36 years old, and I didn't know it. Mum and dad had been divorced since I was a little girl and I had a wonderful relationship with him even if at first it was really difficult for me. I saw him every week and we did a lot of trips together. I can still remember what he told me the night before he left. We were calling each other and he said: "I love you." I answered: "Me too" and he told me: "It is not enough to say me too! It is better to say I love you too" and we laughed about it. It was a great moment, our last moment together. I couldn't say goodbye, it hurt too much, I couldn't believe what was happening.

From that day I sewed me a suit of armour, no one could see my feelings, and no one could see how much I was suffering. Everything was inside me and my life went on with my daily routine. However during the nights, when I was alone, with me and myself only, I could strip off my armour and show my real feelings and thoughts.

Yes, that day, my life changed. I changed. I learned to be strong learned to force myself, to pick myself up, to look ahead. I understood that everything can happen during your life and it is important to accept and overcome problems. Today I know that this experience, even if it was a really bad experience, taught me things that I need for my future life. Now I am more independent and mature than before, so maybe it is for this reason that since I turned 19 years old I live alone with my dog although I have a beautiful and important relationship with my mum and my young sisters. You can take something good out of all your experiences and this is important. I think that this concept can help you to overcome the bad episodes in your life.

Some people want to overcome the snow, just like they do with a bad experience. I embrace the snow, because of this day in which my father had to leave me.

Austria
On the floor

I was sitting on my sofa staring at a wall. I looked at Jimmy Hendrix lying on the floor playing the guitar. I looked at paintings and a comic I drew. There was a lot of stuff on my wall. Every time someone got into my room they were staring at all these drawings, posters and photos. A room full of impressions but I was empty. I felt like a bottle waiting to be recycled. First smashed down, and then put onto a band conveyor ready to melt down in a heating stove. Suddenly my heart started to beat faster. I couldn't breathe and the wall had become awfully big, nearly crushing me…When I was fifteen years old I was empty. I was living in a dark hole, lying on the ground, doing nothing. First the doctors didn't know what was wrong with me. I suffered from cardiac arrhythmias. I got to hospital and they did a lot of examinations but still…I didn't get better. Once a doctor sent me to a psychologist and my journey started…

I was in therapy for almost five years. I suffered from depression and panic disorder. I couldn't go to school. I couldn't go outside. It was even hard to go to the therapy. I only could make it with medication.

My father didn't believe me and didn't listen to what the doctors were saying. He just thought I was lazy and didn't want to go to school. He blamed me for the way I was.

I was always a bit different. Not special or unique just a bit different. When I was in primary school I began to write my own stories. I liked to read, paint or draw comics. I even did a musical and dramaplay. I was (and I still am) some kind of a nerd.

When I was in secondary modern school people started bullying me. Sometimes they locked the doors of the toilets at school. I couldn't go out. Sometimes they were just surrounding me and pouring juice over my head. But I don't want to tell you about the bullying because I'm sick of it and I also think that people are sick of hearing about bullying-stories. Anyways, the interesting part about this chapter is that although I had been bullied in class, I was the class representative for three years.

My parents tried to help me and talked a lot to the teachers but they didn't help me. They thought I was "fine" or they just didn't want to get their hands dirty.

When I was a teenager I felt like a leper. I was alone, I was scared of the world, and I was afraid of people and afraid of the future.

At some point I decided to quit. I decided to quit with being afraid of the world, thinking about the way I looked or the way I was. I decided to live. I started drawing again. I started to write again, to write music and stories.

All of which I've written now seems childish and superficial but still…it was hard to get judged and blamed for being me.

I want to live, I want to feel, I want to explore the world and meet people. I want to breathe, I want to absorb life with all my heart, and when I decided to quit my old life, I started a new one.

What I would read if you wrote me

I wonder...
What I would read if you wrote me.
Would you have come up with the words
that have always been living under your skin?
Would you have built me up with your rare and most dearest silent vowels and consonants
which only echo in your safe and loving appearance?
Will the words have aroused me,
wanting to read more,
more than what I now perceive from the mystery that is yours?
Could one word have had the loveliest sound,
the most outstanding syntax,
the most tender significance?
Will you have written me in my completeness
or will you have regretted the way you held your pen
in the moment your heart was captured on the paper sheet?
Will you have dreamt up, written and rewritten,
eliminated a few letters and filled in the gaps?
Or will I see that what had always been unwritten
at last is more refined than what you could have ever fixed on paper?
Will I treasure the unwritten
like I have always treasured you?
Wipe out the vague scrabbled handwriting,
but scrape along together the a's, b's and c's,
catch them in a petty jar
and mason it in our solid walls.
A white house
with a wooden floor,
the years along with its growth rings.
A cat to play on it and a child to touch it as a safe soil.
This is what we are writing,

this is every unspoken word
becoming a lifetime of sentences
caressing us in the everyday silence.
It is us,
keeping warm together
at the hearth of burning, scribbled paper.

Russia
European dream

"Hi, my name is Iana and I am from Russia, from Siberia" – it was the first phrase I said at the university in Denmark. From exactly this phrase my unforgettable and fascinating studying and living in Denmark began. But my way to this program and to this country wasn't very easy. And it was a long way. I would like to share this story with you.

For us as for Russian students it's rather difficult to get a chance to study somewhere abroad. Especially when you don't live in the center of the country, but in its further part. That is why when we heard about this opportunity, to take an Erasmus course for three months, many students including me inflamed.

It wasn't enough to agree to participate in this program; we had to meet with the approval because there were only two positions. There were two rounds. Both of them took place at our university and were evaluated by our teachers.

The first one included a motivation letter. For me it was very difficult to write it. We had to prove that we want to go here and to explain why. You know it is very confusing to put all your thoughts and feelings together. I was writing the letter during several days, every time I tried to add something, to remember some things. I sent it to my university and after that, I got the next task.

The next round included the presentation on the topic of the project our university was working on. It was "Social integration of minorities. Problems and possible solutions". When I heard the topic, it seemed too complicated for me to make it. I was thinking to refuse. The night before the day we were to present it, I decided to do it. Finally, I thought that the first round was made why not try myself in the second one. So, I was searching for the material and making the presentation right before the deadline! It was a little bit crazy I think. The next day I was very nervous, I thought that everyone would have perfect and complicated presentations and that mine was so short and simple. I had decided to talk as much as possible on the topic but not make a lot of slides in the presentation. The time of presenting was drawing on.

I wasn't the first or the last in the list of participants, I was somewhere in the middle. So even now I remember every minute of my presenting. It was the first time I presented a project in English. It was a great experience for me. I was asked a lot of questions and after that I could be free. My friend said that everybody really liked my project, but I didn't believe her.

Than it was a time of waiting. Everybody was asked to leave the room and wait a bit. When we were invited I was sure they would choose anybody except me! And in five or so minutes I heard my name. It was a shock. I didn't believe it, and finally I felt relief and joy at the same time.

In fact I didn't tell anybody about my participation! After I knew that I won I sent a lot of massages to my mother and my friends. First they couldn't understand what happened and then they were really happy for me!!! When I came home I understood how much my parents were proud of me. So the goal was achieved.

Now I am here, in Denmark, in the happiest country with the best teachers, students, and atmosphere. Now I can divide my life into two parts: before the Erasmus course and after that! I remember that every day before the trip I was dreaming about my living and studying here. I imagined a lot of things. Now I understand everything you can imagine is real. I am happy. Dreams come true. Thank you.

My little world

I wonder how it can be
That when I wake up in the morning I see
A pink little candy tree

The rainbows are yellow
The weather is fine
I don't know the word sorrow
Everything is mine

I wonder how it can be
That when I look out of the window I see
A small flying chocolate bee

The rivers are green
The weather is fine
I don't know the word mean
Everything is mine

I wonder how it can be
That when I open the bathroom door I see
A beautiful blue sea

The flowers are red
The weather is fine
I don't know the word sad
Everything is mine

I wonder how it can be
That when I step out of the house I see
A wonderful world for me

Belgium
A beacon of hope

My story starts the year I entered the 3rd grade of secondary school. The bullying was now going on for 8 years and I was getting more and more isolated. I had no friends, no social life and black thoughts sometimes crossed my mind.

My parents saw me going down and decided that they couldn't bear watching this any longer. We made an appointment at the CLB (Centre for Pupil Guidance connected to the Belgian schools).

I will never forget how I felt when entering that building...

I felt so insecure and nervous at the same time, but most of all, I was afraid of meeting someone from my school because the CLB is where you go if something is wrong with you...

I entered the room of Ms C (the woman who gave the guidance). She started off with some questions. She was testing how far she could go and what the problem was exactly. The next thing she did was test me. Tests for all sorts of things like ADHD, autism and even to see if I was highly gifted. I cannot describe the feeling when you hear that nothing is wrong with you. Unconsciously, you know that you are alright but all those years of bullying leave their marks. You start doubting yourself, you want to change yourself to become popular, and you blame yourself for who you are...That moment the tests say you are no different than the average 15 year old is such a satisfying moment. It felt like a beacon of hope, I can overcome this! Nonetheless, the doubting remains a part of me even until this day.

Now it was time to take action, change doesn't come by itself. I had to take my life into my own hands and do something. Blaming others and losing yourself in self-pity won't take you anywhere. The lady gave me the advice to look for something outside school. Breaking the bubble, finding some friends outside the normal circle and starting with a blank sheet. Looking upon it now, this is probably the best advice someone ever gave me...

I followed this advice and upon this day I'm still active in this youth organization, forever grateful and repaying the debt of pulling me through.

From this moment on, things went better. There were ups and downs but the fact that I had friends outside school really kept me going. I had something to look forward to, not something to be anxious about. I knew that each week would have a good weekend.

Looking in the past, the 3rd year of secondary is not the worst year in my life. In fact it is one of the most important turning points in my life. The year everything started to get better. The isolation left its marks, but time heals all wounds.

Basque Country
Somebody to lean on

I was 16 years old. I was talking with one of my best friends and we were laughing about life. We finally decided we should go to bed, due to the fact that the next morning we had to wake up early to go to school. But at around 12:30 am I received a call I was surprised. It was one of my friend´s boyfriends who was calling me; I answered the phone and he kept telling me his girlfriend called him crying that her mother has died.

We did not know what was going on, so we decided to go to my friend's house. I woke my mum up telling her about the phone call.

My friend's boyfriend and his mother, and my mother and I went to my friend's house to see what was happening. While we were arriving we saw an ambulance just in front of her house and we started to get really worried. We opened the door and my friend was sitting on the stairs, trembling and crying. We took her and when we were going into her house, her father did not know what to do, what to say… he was just disappeared from our world, waiting to hear something from the doctors. In that exact moment the doctor came out of the bedroom and made a "no" with his head. All people who were in that house were shocked, their life was suddenly changed. They had lost a wife, a mother, an aunt, a friend…

We were standing there without knowing what to do. We took our friend to have a little walk, to try to relax a little bit. Meanwhile, I sent a message to our friends, texting what happened.

But the hardest moments were still to arrive. I could not sleep during that night; I was wishing it to be the time I had to get up.

This was the moment when I really realized how much I need my family and friends. When things go wrong we always need someone to be with, to tell what happened, or whatever. Sometimes we do not realize about the persons who honestly we need until we feel they are not next to us.

That occasion also made us to be closer to our friends, and to realize who really loves you and who you care for.

Belgium
Chimeras and delusions

The beginning of the end. At least that's how it feels when I look back to our trip to Crete in Greece. This small island, so beautiful and so warm, like a paradise. This is how it should feel when you go there on holiday. It wasn't like that for me. I'm Jolien. I'm 14 years old and I am fat. At least, that was how I felt. Just a normal day by the swimming pool, you think. One of my many horrible days in a bathing suit with a towel wrapped around my body. Seeing all these skinny girls walking in their bikinis made me feel worse. From my seat in the shadow, I could see handsome tanned boys looking to these girls… I could never be such girl. I was fat and ugly. I had a low self-esteem. Together with my family I spent 8 days in Crete. I can't remember swimming in the pool. What I can remember is this. My father and I went hiking in the 'National park of Samaria '. It is an amazing natural phenomenon. A once-in-a-lifetime opportunity. What bothers me is that the only image that crosses my mind is a picture of me, being all sweaty and … fat. When I look back on this beautiful experience, images of high mountains, little villages, small creeks and fantastic nature doesn't cross my mind. I think you already know what does cross my mind. You see, all my life was about my weight. And it would remain equally so, until I was 18 years old.

The end of my life as it was. My life changed at that moment. A small insignificant moment in which nothing happened. When I close my eyes, I can see myself gaze in the mirror at the airport. I and my family were traveling back to Belgium. Traveling takes time because you have to wait to check in and before boarding. In one of the waiting rooms, there was this really big mirror. You know the kinds of mirrors they have in ballet classes? Right, that kind of mirror! As I was staring at my reflection in the mirror, I made a decision that would change my life…in a bad way.

A new school year begins. My school was taking part in a project named 'Fit classes'. Every student had to take a fitness test, they measured your weight and you length. Everyone was comparing each other's results. I tried to get rid of mine as fast as I could. They say you cannot ask a girl for her weight, well they're right. It was so embarrassing for me to see it, my weight, my fat mass, and black letters on white paper. I don't really know the purpose of this 'Fit class' anymore, but for me it meant a good opportunity to lose weight. So I started running. Just a few minutes around my house was enough to make me gasp for air. But days went by and I kept on jogging. Every day I tried to run a bit longer. At home, I wasn't eating as much as I used to eat. It was still normal though, like a diet. You must know that, 1 year earlier, I tried to go to a dietician. Back then, I wasn't motivated enough to keep this up. I was less mature and it scared me a bit, talking about what I ate in the presence of 10 other people. 3 months passed and in school there was an intermediate weighing. I lost weight! I was so happy. I told my friends and the said they could really see it when watching my face. One day, the sports teacher – who was leading this project – came to me to ask how I was. I was eating an apple and she said: "Is that all you're going to eat?" And I said: "No, of course not!" Back then, I was thinking: "How could she ever think this is all I'm going to eat?" In the end, she was the one that planted a bad idea in my head.

More months passed and I kept running. But this running wasn't satisfying me anymore. I wasn't losing weight fast enough. Instead of running more, I started eating less. There was this one day that I didn't want to get out of my bed in the morning, because then I had to eat breakfast. In my family, everyone leaves the house for school or for work on a different time. So, obviously, everybody wakes up at a different time. These days, I was alone in the morning. This way, there was no social control on what I was eating. Day after day, I ate yoghurt with half a banana. When there's no one to make me eat breakfast, there's also no one while I'm making my lunch for school. In the beginning, it was 2 slices of bread with some lean filling like chicken. After a while, it became one instead of 2 slices. I ended up with only three strawberries as lunch. By this time, my friends at school began to notice I wasn't eating enough. I couldn't stand them saying anything about it. For my standards, I was eating a hell of a lot! If I'm completely honest with you, I was so hungry. But after a while it becomes part of you and you don't notice it anymore. This one day, me and my friends were standing outside on the playground. The weather was bad and I was cold. My new blue winter jacket wasn't enough to keep me warm. My stove didn't get any wood to burn anymore. I was always cold. When I pulled up my shoulders – because I was freezing – the wind could get under my new blue jacket. This way I was even more cold, but I liked it. It meant that my jacket was way too big, even though I bought it only 3 months ago.

The running stopped, so did the eating. I was still so fat! I even couldn't stand the idea of looking in the mirror. At home, I was playing with my food. My plate was 'overloaded' with one tablespoon of mushed potatoes and half a chicory with ham and cheese. I remember asking my mother: "Do I really have to finish this?" After dinner, I stuck to the heating. Not only after dinner, also after school, while watching the television, while I was eating breakfast (remember the yoghurt with the banana?), when I was studying … Always. School was hell for me. I didn't want to go anymore. It was exhausting and cold. The cold was exhausting. All my energy was gone, and I liked it. I lost more and more weight; still I thought I was fat. When may holiday's arrived, my family planned a trip to France for four days. My dad shocked me that day. He told me that I couldn't come if I didn't start to eat more. Why did this shock me? Because, when I think about it now, my parents didn't say anything about my eating behavior or my weight loss before this 'outburst'. Travelling is something I like the most. So can you imagine how deeply rooted my problem was, if I was willing to give up travelling for eating? Eventually I went with my parents to France. This one episode I remember very well. I was sitting in the car with my dad. It was beautiful weather and for once, I wasn't cold. In the morning, I made an agreement with myself: If I ate 'so much' that my belly was hanging over the seatbelt, I'd have to eat less the next day. When I sat in the car, I had to struggle to restrain my tears, because what I didn't want to happen happened. But of course it is normal that your belly is hanging over the seatbelt, I just denied it.

Talking, talking and talking. That's all I had to do. Oh, I forgot something. I didn't talk on my own, no; I talked with three different psychologists. The first one, Mister A, was specialized. He was, as they say, very good in handling girls with anorexia. I didn't understand why I should talk to him. I didn't have anorexia! Ok, I knew something was wrong and had to change, but I didn't feel like I had anorexia. I still don't say 'I have had anorexia', I say 'I lost some weight in a wrong way'. So, Mister A tried very hard to help me get rid of the anorexia. He didn't succeed, as I was thinking I didn't have anorexia. One day, I just ran away and I never came back. But, my parents were not pleased. They had had enough of my silly behavior. So I went to Miss B. Miss B was different, but not in a good way. Each time I was with her to talk, she made me stand on a bathroom scale. Do you have the same weight all the time? In the morning I weigh less than in the evening, don't you? Apparently, she did not understand that. When my weight was only one hundred gram different than the last time she weighed me, she asked me how that was possible... She was so focused on the weight and not on the mental aspect. And again, maybe focusing on the physical aspect is needed when you have anorexia, but I didn't have that. Again, I ran away and I never saw Miss B again. After this disaster, I tried not to talk anymore with people who get paid to talk with people. I hated it, giving these people money for doing nothing. The only thing they did was make me cry, make me feel bad. This is what I thought about Mister A and Miss B for a long time.

Another problem entered my life. Or has it always been there? I don't know, but what I know is that I didn't like it. I still don't like it. I have performance anxiety, or at least, they think I have it. Again, I don't want to call it that way. Actually, I don't know what it is, but it isn't fun, I can tell you that. In the beginning of my fourth year of high school, I changed school. I didn't want to go to school in the first school. I came home crying the first 2 days... My mom thought that it would be better if I changed school. When I think about it now, I didn't really cooperate in that decision. I was running around in my own head, trying to find a way. I must say, changing school didn't help me much with solving my problems. The eating-stuff stayed and the school-stress-stuff became worse. Still I do think that it would have been worse if I had stayed in the first school. When it was clear that 'not talking to someone to whom I have to give money for talking to me' was not working, my mum sent me off to Miss C. She wasn't a psychologist. She was a social worker. I told her about my unwillingness to pay people for talking to me. So, she just said: "Ok, than you don't pay me." Miss C helped me a lot. She didn't focus on the 'thing I don't have'. She talked more about the school problem because she thought these two problems were related: low self-esteem.

I always had difficulties losing weight, but suddenly it was so easy. That's why I didn't want to stop. But I've stopped and I'm proud of surviving it so well. Still I think it is because I didn't really have anorexia. I was nearly there, I have to admit. People with anorexia will never fully get rid of it, people say... I've stopped crying for stupid food a while ago and I feel relieved. I like food and I will always like it. I've never stopped liking it. I'm thinking of doing a baker course. I love it when people eat! In that way, I don't have to feel guilty when I eat. In the opposite, I can't stand it when people don't eat. This is one of the remainders of hopefully the darkest period in my life. I think Miss C was right. My eating-problem and the problems at school are linked with my low self-esteem. I feel like I'm cured from the 'not-anorexia', but the low self-esteem is still there...

I wonder what I'm gonna be

I wonder what I'm gonna be
There are so many girls like me.
But I know, I have special power,
That keeps me going every hour.
I have my aim
This life is game.
I make the rules
Outstrip the fools.
I also know I have a fire,
That let me raise my game much higher
I have my goal
Life builds a wall
I break it down
And win the crown.
And all the time there is a fight
You fight your laziness your fright
You fight yourself you fight the others.
And in this fight you find your brothers.
You win you lose
You get a bruise,
But never stop
To reach the top.
This life is game
This game is gorgeous!

Germany
Wanderlust

Living in a different country all by yourself can be hard or it can be the greatest experience of your lifetime.

I was so sick of the town I was living in, seeing the same old people every day, same things repeating themselves over and over again. I was so ready to move on, to experience something new, something different and also to find out more about myself. To be honest, I was quite miserable the time before my final exams. I couldn't wait for everything to be over so that I could finally leave town. Growing up is so very confusing, trying to be yourself when you have no clue who that actually is any more. I just needed a fresh start, a different view on things.

I didn't tell anyone that I filled out an application for going to America for one year as an au pair. Not until I was sure that it would actually work out did I inform my family and friends. I have to admit that seeing their shocked faces, especially my mum's, was quite satisfactory to me. Most of them told me that they wouldn't be able to do it, which made me feel strong. I was quite sure that I would manage, since I had never been the type of girl that felt homesick. Going away that far for one whole year does sound long at first but trust me; it's true that time flies when you're having fun, especially when you're having as much fun as I had.

I loved my kids so much; they were the sweetest 3 little Indian girls (3, 5 and 7 years old when I arrived). It's true that you are born into your family but those munchkins and I loved each other that much that it actually felt like they were my own kids. My relationship to the host parents was a little different. I also got along with the dad very well but I hardly ever saw him. He had to travel a lot for his work which was also the main reason for the family to hire an au pair. Three kids can be a lot for one mum, especially when that mum is regretting getting them. It's not that she didn't love them, I'm sure she did, she just regretted having so many of them (her own words).

She can be the nicest person in the world but being dissatisfied with your life in general, with your marriage and with yourself can turn the nicest person into a person that hates everything and isn't afraid to show it I guess. It was confusing being around here because sometimes she made me feel like I was really part of the family, almost like the two of us being a lesbian couple raising the girls. Nonsexual of course but with her buying me coffee and other treats. At other times she made me feel like I was the family slave that's worth nothing. I was never sure in which mood she would be the next day, even the next five minutes was nerve-wracking. I also saw it in her eyes that although she knew that she did need help, she sometimes regretted getting me as an au pair. It was the fact that the kids and I got along so well that she couldn't stand, especially when given the choice with whom to stay with the kids picked me over her, which was only logical since she hardly ever spent time with them, unlike me. And if she did, she didn't feel the need to actually do something with the kids rather than being on her phone with them being around somewhere. She never apologized for treating me badly but I was always sure to receive a gift the next day. Like this I got new shoes, new handbags… Just saying sorry would have been cheaper and maybe more sincere but hey, who am I to complain with a closet full of nice gifts.

I also met some very nice friends, mostly other German au pairs though. Sharing such an adventure can really connect people.

There was this one girl that I got along with right from the start, Nicole. Everybody just called her Nici though. She is the sweetest, most sincere person in the world. We started to hang out every day since we also lived super close to each other and we discovered that we shared the same interests. She was always able to pick me up when I felt down because I had another bad day with my host mum. I never had a friend like her before. I was comfortable to talk about every topic with her, she was a good listener. In my family and also with my friends at home we don't really talk about feelings, we also don't hug a lot or show any physical affection. For Nici this was different, she was a very affectionate person, a person that wanted to share her feelings and wanted to know more about mine. A person that needs a hug first thing in the morning to have a good day. It made me feel uncomfortable in the beginning since I was just not used to sharing that much personal stuff but we ended up talking a lot which also helped me to find out more about myself.

But sometimes I felt like she saw me as boyfriend substitute. She had a boyfriend at home that she missed a lot and I did feel like I had to compensate for it.

Since I wasn't used to such a close friendship, it got to a point where it just got too much for me. We were spending all our spare time together and I always feel a little strange when someone knows too much about me. I knew that she would never use anything we talked about against me but I also wanted to hang out with other people more which she didn't seem to be wanting. Just the two of us was enough for her. There came a time where I actually felt a little constricted by our friendship.

Luckily for me, her host family went on a one week vacation with her going with them. Not wanting to sound rude now but I actually look forward to not seeing her for a week. In the beginning it felt good to be away from each other for a little while, to be able to do what I wanted without caring about her feelings, but that week also marked the point that I had my worst week with my host mum. I was normally able to cope with her verbal abuse by simply ignoring it but that week was bad. I don't even remember how she insulted me but it was just so unjust and mean and with Nici gone I didn't even have anybody to tell me that it's not true. I did manage the week but I was relieved when Nici came back, I wouldn't have thought that I'd miss her that much. When she finally got back, I went over to her house and I started to tell her what happened that week. I never cry in front of other people, it just doesn't feel right to me. But that evening tears started rolling down my cheeks. I tried not to let it happen. Honestly I cannot remember crying in front of another person ever before. Of course I did cry in front of my mum when I was little but apart from that I cannot recall any other memory of me crying with another person watching. However that day it was ok, I wasn't even ashamed of my tears. Nici comforted me and made me feel better immediately.

Luckily the following months things never escalated as badly again with my host mum and Nici and I got along even better.

Apart from all the other great experiences I really gained a friend for life, a friend that I can always trust, a friend that I can absolutely be myself with. Thank you!

Birthday Suit

I wonder,
Sometimes I just wonder.
>Why people are so brutal and harsh?
>Don't they realize they destroy lives?
>All they do is judge,
>And treat difference as a smudge
>There was this wise man from Japan
>He once asked:
>"Is blaming difference in our nature than?"
>This question is really unsurpassed.
>They teach us about tolerance,
>They teach us about respect,
>And sure, this is of major importance,
>And of course, something to protect

But I wonder,
Sometimes I just wonder
If it is not really just in our nature
>Are people born like this?
>Are we really that brute?
>After all, we all have a similar birthday suit.
I refuse to believe, that brutality is all life can be
I refuse to believe in the human beast.
I believe in being kind,
And yes, perhaps that might make me blind.

Japan
Remorse

We, human beings, are not completed and can never be perfect, and no one can be an exception. Because of many flaws which we possess, we are supposed to make mistakes and regret them. This story is about something I want to delete in the history of my life.

    I was an elementary school student and had a lot of good friends when every day felt like a fantasy dream in which you noticed that it was a dream but you didn't have to wake up and could stay there as long as you wished. There was nothing I had to be worried about, and even Monday mornings didn't make me depressed. Now I can recall that those were the days when I truly could think that life was worth living and carefully tasting every moment, like when you are served an amazingly delicious dish but can only eat in a small mount. My heart was pure enough to be ignorant about evil which resided inside every human heart. Complete peacefulness remained in my school life. A Sudden change was thrown into my life when a new student was transferred to our class. Our teacher announced this news in a morning homeroom. With a feeling of disappointment from boys, it turned out that the new student was a boy. The teacher called his name, then after a moment he came into the classroom. My first impression of him was "he is an ordinary boy." He was not short enough to be joked about, nor was he tall enough to put pressure on us. As a predictable result of having another ordinary student in the class, we could easily accept him as our new friend. The only difference between him and us was that as he was getting used to the class, he began to manipulate other classmates. He knew how to get into people's minds and make a close connection with them. The connection always included a bit of pressure which seemed to indicate that if one disagreed with him, he would immediately cut one's connection with him. When someone noticed his unusual friendships and thought it was necessary to do something about it, it was too late because he had already build up his little empire in the classroom where a silent fear of ostracism controlled the minds of our classmates. Once the construction of his empire was done, it felt impossible to revolt against him since at that point he clearly held power. I didn't even understand the concept of power and let alone what would happen if a person had power until I saw that some classmates unnecessarily began to flatter him with artificial smiles and tried to be one of those who were quite close to him. They wanted to win his favor and be given a part of his power over the classroom. I thought, however, that their secret purpose was a feeling of security which could assure them that as long as they maintained their position in his empire, they wouldn't need to be afraid of being a victim of ostracism. At that point, most of the classmates seemed to be careful about their relationships with him. I could always secretly sense a fear in the atmosphere in the class, and it was obvious that my school life had completely changed and would never go back to the way it had used to be. Every day became stressful because I had to carefully think about what I should say and what kind of answers he expected in a conversation with him. A month had passed since he came to our classroom. His selfish and authoritarian behaviors were clear enough to make me admit that I was totally wrong about my first impression of him. Though he succeeded in pretending to be a good student for our teacher, he was not an ordinary boy but he was possessed with the nature of a tyrant. As any cruel tyrant did in human history, he chose one of the classmates as the first victim to show the rest of us what would happen if one didn't show him an appropriate attitude. It was a girl who was chosen as a victim and supposed to be an enemy against his empire. She was a normal girl and it was not that she tried to show hostility to him. She just wasn't sensitive enough to notice what was going on in our classroom and what kind of a human being he was. I didn't know exactly why she was chosen as his target, but I could guess that she looked the most indifferent of all classmates in his power or manipulation. I can clearly remember the day when his ostracism was introduced in our classroom. One of my friends gave me a piece of paper which required us to ignore her from that day. If we got the paper and he forced us to do the same thing to her, we would surely show him our rejection, but after his manipulation over a month, our solidarity was extremely weakened. Shamefully enough, no one showed a bit of a willingness to rise up against this cruel order from a little tyrant. No one could talk with her, and on the contrary most of us avoided her. As you can easily imagine, there was no way that she didn't notice this sudden change of our attitude toward her. Her face told me her confusion in the situation, and I didn't think that she could figure out the reason for this treatment because she didn't deserve this at all. It was apparently unfair to ignore her for the ridiculous reason. He was just a little elementary kid who actually could do nothing. At that time, however, I was so cowardly that his dictatorship in the classroom was felt like the whole world to me. No one could know when this would stop, and if the end of the order to ignore her would mean ostracism for her. Anyway, the first priority for most of the classmates was not to become the next victim. I couldn't even imagine how hard it was for her to be treated like this for almost no reason. Day by day, her face got more depressive. Moreover, I, too, was suffering from being in the classroom almost every day. I really wanted to put an end to his dictatorship as much as I wanted to run away from it. As a result, I resorted to do something I should never have done. I secretly prayed for his death every day, and I didn't think I was doing something bad, on the contrary I felt some kind of satisfaction that I was doing the right thing and even tried to recommend this to my friends. Fortunately my prayers didn't work, but after 2 month he was sent to a juvenile training school because of his possession of illegal drugs. Our teacher was really shocked by this news, but our classmates couldn't help telling each other how happy we could be again. Now, I don't know how he is and what he is doing. One my friends told me that he was still in a prison many years ago. I feel that I own him an apology, though he would have no idea about what it's for.

One of the symptoms of imperfection in humanity is that we sometimes have too much confidence in what we are doing, and since it can be so superfluous that we consider us as perfect ones forgetting the fact that we are not perfect.

Part of the world or not I deserve to be happy

I wondered...
What if...
What if I have done the things in another way?
If I had been stronger?
If I had heard you?

I wondered...
Why?
Why didn't I fight a little bit more?
Why did I give up?
Why didn't I trust me?
Why couldn't I stop?
Why did I think it was too late?

I wondered...
When?
When did I decided it was too late?
When did I leave myself falling down and decided to not turn me up?
When did I decided that I couldn't deserve something beautiful and unique? Far from the sights, ruses, patterns...

I wonder...
What?
What did I feel?
What made it so overwhelming?
What made it so difficult?

But suddenly a ray of light made me see that even the darkest things in our heart
could be fixed and has an exit.

I did not believe it at the beginning, but sometimes you just need that spark of light, a smile, a look… and the world makes sense again and once more you become part of it.

Although it still remains difficult to go ahead when you fall,
you know that you'll have a hand holding yours no matter what.

And you discover that there are many reasons in life to get up and to smile.

Slovakia
New house occupation

A change of place where my life story will continue, from the old scenario of city Šahy it was going to be two new scenarios actually. Only the main actors will remain and the others together with the scenes will change. One of them, the more important, our home is the one I will talk about. The second, my school and the boarding house.

It was 2007 and we still lived in our old flat, on the same floor as our grandparents. Me, my mom and Vlado. Vlado is my mother's boyfriend and we all lived in that small one room flat. My room was just a half a room to be exact. And half kind of kitchen, like never actually used for eating. The other room was divided into bedroom and living room. And so as you buy some new accommodation you have to move in.

That day has come and we started packing things from our old flat. My mom took the boxes we had in garage or from our grandparents. We started packing all the things and it was really interesting to see how many things you have. People don't even realize how many stuff they collect through their life and put it in different places. It was hard to start and pick the things that could go on the bottom of the box, not fragile. My mom helped me with this because she as a woman can pack things really well and carefully. I started picking things from the shelves and one after the other putting them into the box. As I filled out the first boxes, or rather as the shelves and places on my desk started to get empty, I had this strange feeling. Leaving your home. Now the places started to get emptier but also the apartment started to look messier then before. All the boxes lying around. It was a lot of work to pack them all and it took quite a lot of time. We loaded the first boxes into the car and on the trail car. We travelled that "long" distance, but we had to drive slowly so we won't break anything. When we arrived at the new house it was only about unloading the boxes from the car but we still left the things inside. Then we had to carry the heavy stuff like the washing machine, wardrobes, shelves, fridge and so on... Good that one of the neighbors helped us. He even sat on the trail car on the way to the village so the fridge and mattresses wouldn't fall down. It was dangerous and lucky that the police didn't catch us. Now when you arrive with the heavy stuff you also have to carry it up. That was really hard and took us and the neighbor, plus mom and grandma. Especially carrying some very big sofas. These processes took more than one day and the arranging of the things, not even the small ones but only the big wardrobes and so on, took really long. It was a hard work but at least we had good weather and nothing got wet on the way. Again you realize how many things you have when you have to put them back in their place. It was a big journey to move from the flat to the new house and very, very tiring. But we managed to do it slowly, step by step.

It took a good week until everything was moved to its place and we actually had another real home. I got used to it quite fast; I have my own room now which is very cool.

The whole moving to the new accommodation thing can be pretty stressful. In the end that's life, it is not about being a statue, stationary, solid, but it is about change and being flexible to what life offers you.

Basque Country
One of those special people

We were 8 years old, when my friends and I were bothered by some of the pupils of my school after the physical education lessons. They used to take our belongings (school bags, trousers...) and threw away into the shower. So every time we went into the dressing room we got mad but we couldn't do anything because they were older than us and we were afraid.

That situation was unsustainable. No one knew nothing about that situation, but I felt sad and I decided to tell everything to my sister (that person in which I trusted and nowadays I trust the most).

I don't know what I was thinking by telling her the situation, knowing that she couldn't do anything to defend me, without mattering the consequences.

So the next day she approached the leader of the group and she had an argument with her. Finally, the girl stopped bothering me and from that moment my belongings have never been touched again. And it was then when I understood that small details make a big difference.

I didn't realize in that moment how fortunate I was to have a sister like her. But nowadays I feel the most fortunate person in this world and I am very proud of her.

She is one of the most important persons in my life. She has made me live many of the most beautiful and happiest moments of my life. I've been treasuring each moment; feeling and memory lived with my sister in my heart. Every minute with her is one different story and every feeling is an event. She is strong, kind, she cares for others, she is smart, funny and her smile is able to stop my world.

Every time I think about her I realize that even in this moment there is 7,221,092 people in the world, she is one of those special people I need in my life.

Take your Pencil

I wonder…

If birds feel freedom
If clouds feel peace
If love is real
For human beings

We are intelligent
We can learn
We have feelings
In our hearts

We are supposed to be rational:
We are able to choose!
Make our own decisions
Solve the problems too…

So…

It makes me wonder…
Why can't we live in peace
Care for the others
And don't just live?

It makes me wonder…
Why can't we feel the pain
Worry about it
And make a change?

It's up to everyone
And everyone writes his life
Take a pencil
And write a smile!

Switzerland
In a men's world

"That's a woman, she shouldn't be here!" That was his sentence. That was the first sentence I heard in the shooting gallery. I was shocked by this sentence. Why couldn't I have a chance to be a good shooter only because I'm a woman? No matter what they said. I wanted to try it and prove to them that a woman can be as good as a man if not better than them. I lay down on the floor with my rifle. My godfather was next to me to help me because it was the first time I was shooting. I did a great job. I had really good results. I was really proud to prove to them that a woman can be as good as they are.

I trained again a lot of times and decided to join a team of young shooters. The first time I was there the only thing I wanted was to shoot. But I quickly learned that it is not so easy as it seems. You can't come in a shooting range and just pretend to shoot. You have to learn a lot of things for it to be safe and have good results. The first important thing we learned was the security rules. I also had to learn to quieten, to clear my head and focus on nothing else than the target. Breathing is really important for us. To make a good shot you need to breathe really slowly almost without moving. To be structured while I'm working with weapons and to be self-confident were also really important lessons.

It was sometimes really hard because the other young people were often telling me that I just had to close my mouth because I was a woman and that I had no power. But no matter I wanted to shoot and I wanted to prove to them that I could be as good as them. The first lessons I went there I learned how to be with them and how they were acting with me. Then I stopped let tingthem walk over me. In the beginning it was really hard I had to find a way to be respected in this man's world. I was a quiet good shooter so I used my results to get respect from them.

At the end of the first year there were the results of the whole year. What a great feeling it was to be the first of the first year group and to be the only girl. I was really proud of it. Happiness is not enough to describe how I felt at that time. I was used to be the last one in sport and never the best in the class, the normal girl smart enough to have no problem but not the best.

After three years, I decided to become a kind of teacher for the next young shooters. I wanted to give them all the pleasure and the quietness that shooting could bring you. I was not pretending to be the best or the worse I only wanted to be who I am and no matter if I am a woman I can also do what I want.

It brought me a lot of things like friendship, laughs, self-esteem but also doubts. Because when you're a good shooter you are taking part in tournaments and you have this competition spirit to get good results and always be better. It makes you doubt and those doubts are afterward making you a more self-confident person.

Actually I have gained respect from them but not in the way I hoped. They respect me and know I can be really good. But they are not considering me like a woman. A sentence was really important and stays in my mind: "It's normal you get good results. You are a lady boy. A man stuck in a female body."

Slovakia
My life experiences

I was born in 1991 – 2 years after was a big change – Czechoslovakia separated to Czech Republic and Slovakia. My life begun quietly, but the silence ended very fast. I have had quarrels with my younger sister – so I remember my first slaps on my face from my father. It was unfair. I still remember the marks. I could forgive him, but sometimes I can't forget it. I try my best to forget he bad memories, and remember about the good things. After my sister started to go primary school, then I was in kindergarten. I hated it. My parents pulled out from there. I was happy. I loved my mother very much. My sister was jealous of me. My first primary school arrival I was crying, because I was scared to leave my mother. My grandpa brought me from Tesmak (village) fresh warm cow milk. These years were so wobbly. My grandparents brought me up. Later my mother was very busy at teaching, and my father worked in borders, like frontier-guard.

Before I went to school my grandmother taught me about our religion. I prayed a lot for my God and sang together. I served there. Some people said that I would become a priest someday. In school I studied slowly my first foreign language at the age of 6. I hated it, but I endured with all my will. My teachers were warmhearted. I remember my primary school teacher. She passed away a few years (7) ago. I think she was one of my favorite teachers. When my younger brother was born, we played a lot at home. He was my best friend. I helped him a lot. We usually saw drama films, action films, comedies with famous actors: Jackie Chan, Hwang Jang Lee, Yuen Wo Ping, Jet Lee, Bruce Lee, Donnie Yen, John Liu Tino Wong. I liked to go outside with my new friends and classmates. We played roll play games, we acted like we had a camp, a secret base, where we can play cards, share our good experiences and be happy together. That small group dismissed after we entered the secondary school. We separated to 2 groups. Gymnasium – the smartest kids in secondary school, and base school the weakest ones. After we reached puberty, we tried to find a group where we can enter. New life began. We bought a computer; I started to communicate with my friends in Skype. I played a lot computer games, I was quite addictive to Final fantasy game series. I joined to the singing chore. We sang a lot together. Also I joined to the town singing chore too. My hyperactivity appeared in sports, especially soccer, volleyball, basketball, athletics and martial arts. I couldn't behave always in a good way. I had problems in the school once. I endured a lot of harm. I kept participating in singing events in abroad – Budapest, Galánta etc. – and join to the school trips together with other classes. I never forget the trip to High Tatras, where we were skiing, playing gin forest, and forest running. We also went to a swimming trip. I remember my classmate colored his hair full dark blue. These were fun. I also went to a tour with my cousins. During summer breaks in my father's home place, in a small village we met with my grandparents. Grandmother helped me to learn how to cook a good jelly in summer. We worked together in garden fields. We had a lot of fun, eating grapes, to harvest and to make wine with my cousins. We also played in pubs, and drank beers. I started to drink at the age of 16. I always kept the line. I never was drunk. Concerts in advent – our catholic religion had good events together in the church. We sang a lot – spirituals, Latin German and English songs. I noticed at the time of my 17th birthday that I had some problems in my body. My grandmother went with me to the hospital, and the doctors pulled out my big mother mark from my back and from my chin. Also they removed my though skin from my feet. I walked wrong when I was younger. After I get cured, I fell in love with one cute girl. I started to make poems. I wrote 80 poems in a row in a small diary. She burned them all. The love was one-sided. I finished my exams in school. I had good grades. My last party with my classmates was in the dining room at the school. We danced a lot together, and our class-band played in drums, guitars, etc. It was awesome. My parents got divorced. My mother was beaten by my father. I successfully joined to university in abroad, in my 2nd home country, in Hungary. I studied medicine.

After a year I failed to finish because of Physics. I worked in Vác for 8 month. I made Smartboards in Zollner Factory. I heard from others, that my German teacher died in cancer. After a few years my grandmother shared the same fate. I helped her to survive many hardships, so she was my first mother, friend, teacher, priest and so on. I wanted to ask her many questions about the life, but it seems I need to look after answers alone.

My current state is at the Apor Vilmos College in Vác, where I met with my girlfriend. We are together two and half years ago. Every weekend I'm going home to meet with my grandfather, brother and mother. My sister and I have average relationship, so I try my best to get along well with her. My father still works in Norway, in salmon factory. I tried to participate on the Erasmus course, and I became lucky enough to get in.

FREEDOM AINT FREE

I wonder how it would be

I wonder how it would be
when you would see

how I'm now
I'm so different, wow

I'm trying to be strong
this is why I write this poem

I hope it will help me
but this we will see

I wonder how it would be
Or if I should let it be

I will come back home
But how will it go?

I would like to see my future
A close and fantastic future

I wonder why she chose me?
I would like to know it

I have lot of questions
But I don't have answers

Will I live abroad?
I would like to know

I would like to know
But, sometimes, is better the unknown.

Slovakia
The animal shelter

I have a dream. I have a dream that one day I will have an animal shelter for abandoned or not wanted animals.

Long time ago, well, to be more specific it was 15 years ago, my life changed. I didn't win a lottery, I didn't see UFO, and neither became a child movie star. When I was four or five years old I wanted to have a dog, as almost every child, but my father was strictly against it. We have been living in a house with a garden but it wasn't that big. But at least, my neighbor had a small dog, Rundy, which could get under the fence and we secretly played in my garden. Sometimes, when I got meat and rice for lunch, I took it outside and I shared it with Rundy. He got the meat and rice was mine. But as months were passing, I really started to think that I will never get my own dog. But then it was my 6th birthday! And do you know what I got? Well, I don't remember but it wasn't a dog. Two months later my godparents came to visit us. I was brushing my teeth in the bathroom when I heard that they are outside talking with my parents. I didn't rush, I had time to finish brushing my teeth, but suddenly I heard a dog barking. I was sure it was not Rundy, the barking sounded differently. I spat the toothpaste out and run outside. And there she was. A beautiful, brown and white spits-dog puppy. She was running through the whole garden and discovering the new home. I didn't want to have lunch that day; I just wanted to play with the dog. She didn't have the name yet, so it was up to me to pick it – she is Linda.

We spent a lot of time together, I was teaching her to sit, stay, give a paw, lay down or "dance". I must say she was pretty clever. My father started to like her as well, but it took some time, well, let's say years. When I saw he is not furious about the dog at home I slowly started to bring other animals. Three years after, I wanted to save a cat, which should be killed, because the owner had many kittens. So I rescued at least one. And during the next ten years I had around twelve more cats. Some I found abandoned at the cemetery, some were meowing on our trees and when I put them down they decided to stay with us and other were "kids" of my previous cats. It's nice to see how animals change people. Two years ago something incredible happened. My father brought one small puppy at home. One of his colleagues had a lot of puppies she wanted to give away so he wanted to help. I was really surprised and pleased for what he had done.

I also took care of some birds that fell down of the nest, until they were able to fly again, and also about the squirrel that was abandoned, but she was too small to survive without mother. When I was leaving home and travelling to Denmark, we have been taking care of two dogs and two cats. But last week we got a new member of the family. Kids from the poor family probably didn't have enough money to take care of the puppy, so they came with their mother to our gate and left him there. My parents gave him some food and he was really grateful. He also gets along with other furry friends very well.

So in fact, my dream came true. I have a small animal shelter. We have never bought any of our dogs or cats. We just took those who needed help or those that were not wanted in their families. I think we often forget how it is to have pets. They might be only a part of our life, but for them, we are all for them, the only person in their whole life.

People (1)

I wonder...
About my old life
About my new life
About my life

I wonder...
Why the birds fly
Why the flowers grow
Why we change

I wonder...
About my answers
About my no answers
About my heart

I wonder..
Why we want to know what will happen
Why we need to believe
Why...
Because you cannot wait for your future
Because your future is you

Belgium
Tuesday, the 7th of September in 2010

My story starts with an ordinary 250th day of the year. I get out of my bed, take a shower, have breakfast and go to school. It is the second week of my last year in high school and I am planning to kick some ass before College.

After a normal, sunny day at school, I come home and drop my stuff in my room like I always do. I lie down on my bed for a few minutes because school often makes me tired, certainly after 2 months of travelling and having fun. I take my Ipod on and try to relax.

17h23.

I hear my mom coming home from work. She's a little bit later than normally, but still on time. While she is hanging her jacket in the closet in the hallway, I hear her shouting: 'Hey Sara, I'm going to start cooking already because I'm a little bit late today'. "Ok mom, I'll come and help you in a minute! I am just packing my bags for the music school." It will be my first lesson at the music school so I am excited.

17h33.

Only 10 minutes later. I've packed my bags for the music school and I'm heading downstairs to help my mom with making dinner when I hear the telephone ring. "Mom, can you take it, please?" She didn't answer, but I knew she took the phone call because it stopped ringing. My music is still playing.

"We can never go home…We no longer have one."

Oh god, I love the acoustic version of 'No Sound but the Wind' from Editors.

I am just on the stairs when I hear a pan and knife falling on the ground. I run of the stairs as fast I can, because I thought my mom had fainted. When I open the door of the living room, I see her sitting in the sofa, crying like a little child, with the phone still in her hand. "It can't be true", she said.

I can feel in my stomach that there is something seriously wrong.

'Sara, I think that it's better if you sit down for a second. There's something with Anton.' I will never forget her face when she spoke these words. There is not much to tell. Anton, my favorite cousin, died in a work accident. He is turning 19 on the 16th of September.

I'm staring in front of me. Not thinking, not speaking, just staring into the greatest darkness I've ever known until now.

"He can never go home, he no longer has one…"

I feel weak, powerless and everything hurts like hell. I have one hour before my course at the music school begins. I still want to go, but my mom thinks that it would be better if I stay home and wait for my dad and sister to come home from work. The next few hours are one big black whole, but it was the first time that I saw my dad crying. My sister didn't say a word and went to the horses immediately.

This sunny 250th day of the year turned out to be the most darkest one I've known until this day.

After dinner, I went upstairs to lie down in my bed. My dad has to take my arm because I can't walk properly. I try to sleep, because I have to go to school the next day, but I can't. Every time I close my eyes, I see his face.

The next morning: It was just a dream

I am planning on going to school today, because I need some distraction. My father decides to go with me because he is afraid that I won't make it to school. Nobody at the school knows about what is going on because I asked my parents not to call the headmaster. Only my closest friends know about the death of my cousin and my relation to him. At first, I feel good because I am surrounded by my friends. But soon I started to realize what really happened yesterday. This day, is the hardest day of my school carrier. When I came back home from school, I couldn't stop crying because I didn't want to believe what was going on. I took my phone and called Anton more than 10 times.

No answer. Because he didn't pick up his phone, I decided to send him a message. No answer. For the following week... No answer.

The funeral

It has been one week now, since he died. It's my mother's birthday today, and also Anton's funeral. I know that it will be a hard day for me. My mom has taken some pills for her heart and we're making ourselves ready for the funeral. I look good from the outside, but inside I'm feeling miserable, or even worse than the word 'miserable' can describe.

The way to the church has never been so long before. Right before we arrive at the church with our car, Editors' "Papillon" is playing on the radio. It gives me the power and strength to go out of the car and walk into the church. It was the last push in my back I needed, my last sprinkle of courage. The church is way too small for all the people who want to say goodbye and I feel really uncomfortable with all the unknown faces staring at us. They look like they are all showing their grief to us; but honestly, I have already enough grief myself. I take a seat in the front, sit and wait. I can't look at my family because it's too hard to see them suffer. Seeing my grandparents cry is one of the most touching things I've ever seen. His best friends and colleagues are carrying his coffin. They put him down, right next to me. My heart starts to beat faster, my stomach is beginning to hurt and I start to sweat heavily. I'm not feeling well. Luckily they began soon, so I could concentrate on something else. They are telling a lot of things about him. I try not to cry. And I kept myself together, until I saw 3 friends of me who skipped class to come to the funeral. I collapse for the fifth time this week. My mother tries to make me stop but it's just getting worse. I feel stupid. I don't want to cry in front of people I barely know, but still I do. The ceremony is over. My uncle has to carry me out of the church because I can't feel my legs anymore.

I want this day to be over. I want everything to be over... I wish it all didn't happen.

Papillon

During the whole funeral, I sang "Papillon" in my head, over and over again. It was stuck in my head, for no reason.

When I first visited his grave for the very first time, I wrote a text to put on his gravestone trying to express how I felt:

'Human life is too short, that's a fact we can't deny. But one thing I know for sure… You, Papillion, will always fly.'

The moment that I putted the text on the stone, there was a beautiful butterfly sitting on his gravestone. It might have been coincidence, but for me it wasn't. It was a sign from him. It told me that Anton is still among us.

From this moment in my life, I lost my belief in God. From this moment, music helps me to carry the fire. From this moment, butterflies are 'my precious'. Because of this all… everything changed. I changed.

An Angel in Exile

I wonder how to learn more about love
Two hearts were fluttering in separation
So there was sadness and longing
Only to tie us hand in hand together.

I shall strain you to my heart,
Whisper softly in your ear,
How I want to be loved
Every day for many years.
So much more I have to say
And I will, but not today.

In my dreams you rarely smile
Often sadness dims your eyes,
You're like an angel in exile
From celestial paradise.
Don't be sad, I won't delay,
I will come, but not today.

Today is cold and I'm alone,
Lying under a pile of blankets,
Trying to keep my body warm
And my mind out of the surroundings.
Real life invites me in,
But I'd rather sleep and dream.

Belgium
I See Tears

From primary school I was picked on. From the first year. I was a chubby so I was an easy object for bullying. I also didn't have real friends in primary school, so I was an easier object to bullying. In the beginning, my parents tried still to help me by going to the school and tell it to the teachers. Of course, they gave this up after a while too.

For example, I was now in the 5th grade. It had snowed and the roads were very slippery. On the sides of the road were still pieces of ice. I was cycling at home alone. But at a crossroads right before I had to drive into my street for no reason some kids in my class block my way. They took some of the ice balls and began to throw them at me. I could not avoid it in the beginning but after a while it began also to push so I fell off my bike in the middle of the intersection. There was a car coming. This could just brake in time. The kids were just laughing along. I then just drove on home. 200m further these children were waiting, again with ice balls. One of the balls hit my eye. I'm definitely lying in pain for 10 minutes. When I got home I told the story to my parents but they were not shocked at all anymore and just did nothing, just told me that I should learn to defend myself. Of course, doing this gave even more pain.

It was not just on the bike that I was bullied. Many of these guys were in the football club where I played soccer. At every training-session I was always bullied, every time. I remember one time the boys had pushed me so hard that I fell against the heating hurting with my knee. I had a very large open wound. When the coach asked what had happened, everyone said I fell against the heater. What could I say then?

Also on the playground, at the time, almost always the boys played football. But of course I could hardly compete here just because these were the same people who picked on me again. So I usually was thinking why am I actually so fat, why were they always picking on me? On a bench, after only playtimes, there were so many other guys, so many other people who could bully.

I hoped things would improve as I met new people in secondary. But the opposite was true, some children who were in elementary school with me, also went to the new school, and they made more friends than me. And so very quickly it all happened again here. It was the same story all over once again – I was bullied.

But I survived, even though these years were really bad for me.

Say goodbye to a person, who is still alive
This poem is about my grandmother, who has dementia on an advanced stage.

I wonder how a soul can leave,
but the lungs still breath?
You never know, if somebody's here,
or from the earth already disappeared.
For a moment you will wait,
then you know nobody stayed.
All of the sudden it comes to your mind,
There is not your beloved person, she has already died.

Am I a bad human, when my love is not that strong anymore?
Or is it just the answer of my grief what I don't ignore?
Am I in the stage of acceptance?
Or do I want to get in distance?
Am I just waiting for her death?
Or do I want to feel more than only the person's breath?

What shall I do with the person in front of me?
It's like looking for the end of the sea.
She doesn't know who I am,
I can't crash this unbreakable cover of a bar clam.
Can I still love this person from the deep of my heart?
I can also see it as a new start.

But I still wonder how a soul can leave,
but the lungs still breath?

Spain
A real goodbye

Everything began with my grandparents' immigration to Switzerland many years ago. My father lived there for seven years, and during that time he made really good friends, amongst them, Serge.

Over the years Serge became a real friend to my dad, like a brother. When I was six months I met him, his wife and their two sons. They were like my family.

Years passed, we went to Switzerland, they came to visit us, I learned French to be able to speak with them. During Christmas 2001 we received the news, María, Serge's wife had cancer. Cancer was widespread, there was no going back... just survive, as long as she could.

The summer arrived and my parents and I went to the North of Spain for our holiday. During the trip, Serge called again. Time was running out, and she wanted to say goodbye. My parents wanted me to stay at home because I was only 11. This trip was going to be a hard experience. Serge insisted that I went too. *"Toni, Maria veux aussi dire adieu! à Térésa."* The next day we arrived in Hérémence.

It was a hard week, but especially the sincerest "goodbye" I've ever said. It will be forever.

I'm not going to say that this experience changed my life then, I was too young for that ; but I'm sure, I learned with it and all these emotions made me live my life in a special way.

We organised a party for her, a farewell party. The party was in a small wooden house in the middle of the wonderful mountains of the Alps. María spent the day with us. She was enjoying every detail, she knew that it would be the last time she would see it all.

That night she talked to me, she requested me to enjoy the small details "don't waste your time, you have to observe and enjoy everything". And now this is my life, *sitting in a train station watching the people and inventing their lives; reading, sitting under a tree enjoying the breeze, breathing deep whenever something smells good.* She also taught me a French word "chat" (cat)

The same night Serge spoke to me but I can't remember the conversation clearly. My French was not too good, and there were many emotions together. But I remember his face: pain, happiness, all together in the same person. He thanked me for being there, for being so strong, so special.

I believe that since I spent those days, I have a favourite place in the world, this garden, these views, the mountains of the Alps, full of peace and quiet and a thousand details to memorize and enjoy.

Belgium
What doesn't kill you makes you stronger

Now I've to write, write something… write something about your own life. Normally I shouldn't be scared to write letters. It's just black letters on a white paper. It looks so easy to do it, just move my fingers on the keyboard from my computer. I wrote a lot of letters on different papers and I was never afraid to do it. But now it's different. I've to tell something about myself, but not just 'daily stuff'. I think I'm afraid about what these letters, this short text, can do with me. Or maybe just because I even don't know if it will do something with me.

When they asked me first to write something about my life what had or has a big influence, then there were different thoughts and experiences in my head. It's strange when I think about things in my life that had an influence on me, are almost all bad or sad things. 'What doesn't kill you makes you stronger', a sentence that a lot of people use, but it's also a big truth. It's almost always that bad things can change more in your life then joyful things.

The text above just shows my fear to write, because I know that it can be harder for me. I know that there are a lot of pent-up feelings. Some of them are deep in me; others are just stuck in different places of my body. At this moment, I feel something in my belly. It makes a weird sound, because this is more than just black letters on a white paper from me.

It's strange how people can change in such a short time. A few years ago- and now I talk about less than five years ago- we were a happy family. I have one big sister, where I did and shared everything with, one big brother, where I could laugh everyday with. My parents still loved each other, even after 25 years of marriage. When we went to the sea or just walked around, they always hold each other's hand, it was almost like they just fell in love! Or this was what other people in our environment thought…

Little by little, they didn't hold each other's hand, they even didn't kissed each other when they left or they came back home. I remember the face of my father, when my mother every time tried to do something good for him. When she came back home, she kissed him on his head. His eyes were so strange, it was like another man. I couldn't see the 'love' anymore in his eyes. At the same moment, I saw the disappointment and despair in my mother's eyes. I could feel everything she felt at the moment, because it was so clear what she thought. Instead of the feelings from my father... For me, it was frustrated, because I couldn't do anything. I could just watch how the situation was, how the pain in the eyes was...

The day that they didn't even sleep together anymore, was really strange. First, they gave a lot of reasons for it. At the beginning, I just believed and trusted them in what they said. After a few weeks and months, it was clear that all of the reasons were just white lies. This was also one of the beginnings from a series of lies. They always said us that they don't tolerate when we should lie to them or other people. Why did they do it to their own children? Not a white lie, it started with white lies, it ended up with infidelity. While I'm writing this short text, there is just one question the whole time in my head 'Why?'... On everything I wrote, I can't explain why these things happened. I just don't know the answer and I know that there should be an answer. I think this is also one of the reasons why I have difficulties to think, talk or feel about the whole situation. I want answers, but I will never have them. I will never know why everything changed my life in a short time.

In the beginning, there were a lot of discussions when I was home. And every time there was a discussion, I just ran away, because I find discussions just reasonless. Sometimes it's interesting, but if it's about something where you can't give an exactly answer about daily life, than it's just waste of time. I didn't care about it and I thought it was normal. I think that it was also normal, because every family have discussions about daily reasonless stuff. My brother always ran away when a discussion started, because he really hates it and he said that it was 'stupid' to discuss about this. My sister was most of the time in her house when the discussions took place. So she was out of all the discussions and sometimes she didn't realized what happened at home, with her family.

But then, there came a big discussion, a discussion that took years before they give a common answer. Even after the years, it was just like two dogs that continued fighting for nothing. The discussion began by my father's birthday. That should be a happy story now, isn't it?! But when my father wanted to go to the football – you've to know that he was a really big basketball fan in the past – with my neighbor, everything started. My neighbor went already for a few years to a famous football team. My mother didn't care about it, because we did a lot with these neighbors. The children were like a brother and a sister for me. I know them since the girl was born. We always played together. There was no week that passed without playing in the garden or somewhere else. Even if we were bigger, we also had a reason, especially in the summer that we sat together to talk or have a barbecue. But when my father said that he wanted to go to another football team – the team where the wife of my neighbor was fan of – then it was really strange for my mother and for us. My mother couldn't understand 'why', because she didn't expect that. When my mother said that, then everything began. It was not his fault, she was just jealous…. Or that was what he said anyway. Good as my mom is, she gave him the present so that he could go every week to the football – two hours away from home – with another woman. Sometimes I asked myself what should happen when she shouldn't give him that conscious present. It was a poisoned present that caused that people started to talk about the, the lies were invited and the frustrations came out. That one (stupid) present made everything broken. And it was not like just a discussion, it made two families completely broken. By this situation, nine people would be changed and broken. At that moment, I saw what happened and I felt totally desperate. I tried to keep myself and to be who I was, but that was not easy anymore. They always say that your parents have to be equal for a child, that you may have no preference for one of them. But at the moment that you stand in the middle of your parents and see what is going on, than you don't have the chance to see them equal to each other. The 'love' that I had for my father, began to change into distrust. I couldn't trust him anymore and I didn't know what he meant to me…

On 30 November 2012 everything changed for me. It was the day that all the bad things and discussions stopped. It was time for a new life, a more quiet life where I don't have to think what I could say or do. On that day my father left our house and moved to another one, in another village near by our city. The week before, they told me that he should move out and I expected that from months before they told it to me. So when he finally was gone, I felt very relieved, because I could breathe again in my own house.

After a while, I couldn't trust my own father anymore, because I knew that he was lying the whole time. Like when he said something that he did, than we discovered that it was not true. When he said that he was walking in our small city and came back after more than two hours, than you know that there is something wrong. I could feel everything around me and I couldn't do anything. When you know that your own father is lying to you about what he's doing or what he wants or what he feels for your own mother, than I even don't believe him in what he feels for me. Does he actually love me? Do you love someone from your own blood you blame for and lie to?

Maybe it has to be better since that day, but until today, I'm not sure about it. The only thing I do know, is ask myself everyday: Why? What if… A lot of questions where I can't answer, not even when I write everything down.

Future

I always look forward to the future
Why..
Because the past is sometimes too hard to look back to
We all made mistakes and the future gives us a change
A change to rewrite those mistakes
We never know what is going to be in a second, minute or hour
It is a mystery for me, you and every person a life

The future fascinates me a lot
Why…
It is something I keep dreaming of every second of the day
Strange that the words I have written here are already made in the past
Just a minute ago this page was white, no writing and no words to be seen here
One thing you can know about the future
That is that you will try not to make the same mistakes like in the past
Here I am writing sometimes about the future
And all I think about is the past

Forward we go
Why..
I can see it in all the things in daily life
I never see anyone walking backwards to their work or home
I never see anyone speak backwards to someone
We can't predict the future but only accept it when it is laying in the past

Time goes so fast

Wind

Reflexes of light on the waves.
Wide swings of landing birds.
Stones.
Clouds, trees and cemeteries.
Feathers like snowflakes in the grass.

Running, running, running.
Stones on my heart.
Where is home?
And what am I supposed to do?

I am a bird now.
Flying instead of running.
Life from a higher perspective.
Being free.
At least till the wind comes to carry me away.
I am wondering to where it will bring me?

Spain
The Meadow

It was the first time I saw my father crying. I was in my bedroom listening to music like any other day, without knowing that it was going to be my last colorful minutes for a long time. He opened the door, and with a trembling voice pronounced the words in tears that I will never forget: Víctor, the mom has cancer. He couldn´t hold back the tears, and went away. I said nothing. I just ran to my mother and hugged her for minutes, while repeating the same words again and again: Why, why you... My mother was diagnosed the 24th of June with ovarian cancer in an advanced state with a tumor of 17 centimeters.

I had never feared death as those days. They were days of fear and uncertainty. Whole days without talking to anyone or leaving home. Grey days and bitter nights.

Before entering the operating room the next week, my mother held my hand and told me that she was going to do everything as possible, that she was going to fight with all her might for me, because she loved me.

The surgery went well, but days later the analysis confirmed that the cancer had spread, and required another surgery. All this coincided with exams time and all my future plans disappeared, but I did not care. I only cared about one thing, I only cared about my mother, and my only task was not to lose hope and fight together.

Before all this happened, the relationship between my parents was getting worse, and my mother was immersed in a depression for quite some time. That worried me. My relationship with my parents had diverged increasingly in recent years. Embracing my father, or holding the hand of my mother after waking up from anesthesia, made me remember the past, and I realized how much I love them.

With time and chemotherapy my mother improved her health. In January of the next year I came to Denmark, where I am now, to study as an Erasmus student for 4 months. Two weeks ago she told me that the analysis had gone fine, and there were no cancer remains in her body.

I feel alive every time I see her smile through Skype, and her hair growing up slowly, like flowers reappearing in a meadow devastated by fire. I love you mom.

Russia
Johnny

Probably all of us in life have a person which could change the rest of people. But unfortunately, you don't speak with him, cause he died or literary hero or he forgot about you a million years ago. You don't go a walk together, don't call each other and don't congratulate with birthday, but you speak with him every day, tell about the most important and less in your life... And by virtue of this you feel a comfort in soul. You feel happiness.

Johnny is such a person. He lives at outside of me and I speak with him every day, I think about him and I reminisce of us.

Our first conversation was about my favorite perfume, he told me that it for elder woman, I should change it, but I laughed and said that the age didn't matter and the most important how you feel yourself inside of you in spite of figures in your passport.

He called me a little child and said to be a more serious, but I think that he liked his role of teacher. The most of his advices are really good for using them in the life. I remember each word.

Well, I think that I should tell about my Johnny.

He is a tall, handsome man and has wonderful eyes. He likes a football, a good music, a women and bdsm. He likes to beat women, make them feel humble and use his cruelty... He said me about this when I called him a very good man. It was really didn't matter for me. Why did I think about it? It didn't regard of me and he has really nice person for me. I've needed just his attendance in my life.

He told me about his life and it was really unusually for me. And I was so proud that I could knew it, that he trusted for me. I wouldn't like to write about this, cause it very personal information.

He said me that I very good and gentle child that I should to be more careful and that he didn't want to "play" with me. Maybe it was a reason of his "take French leave." He left me. He nothing said. It was a big cruelty. When he left, I understood that I love him.

Belgium
My story

I was laying in my bed, again. This time it was worse than yesterday. Couple of minutes ago I was still fine, sitting on the table with my parents because all my brothers were at school. But now everything is dark around me even if I open my eyes.

It feels like there are screams in my head. I close my eyes again, harder this time, trying not to yell and wishing it will be over soon. Time to flip my pillow and press my head against the cold side, it helps for a minute. But the screams are still in my head.

Where is he?

Laying in his bed.

Again*? He is just acting you know, he just doesn't want to go to school, if it was me..*

We don't know that.. and it is not you alone you know..

What would you do then, tell me, I've had enough of it. *Tomorrow he is going back to school!*

"Silence"

It is not my fault I have migraine father, it was not my choice to be laying in bed today and leave all my friends at school. I like to go to school and mother knows that, you don't..

How did it all start.. It was my second year at secondary school, doing Latin.. against my will but you don't want to hear that. Every time if I talk with mother she listens, you don't..

I always wanted to go to sports school, I didn't want to stop with football. I listened to you and went to Latin. On that time I also wanted to go because you said I could do it. The first year it was fine, first in the class like you wanted to. Yet my request that I wanted to play football again was rejected, school goes first. But if there is nothing that follows up to school..

"What's that noise?" There were more screams and it was not from inside my head.

I can't understand them, probably they are in the living room further away from my room. But I can tell it is nothing good. It is the first time I hear them yelling at each other, well not my father, but my mother was also rising here voice.

It is enough..

"What is enough? Please let me know, is it me? I want to do my best, really, I know how important it is for you that I study hard, be the best and make you proud, I want to do it for you but right know I just want to run away from the pressure."

Everyone is sitting in the room, all my brothers were together. My mother began to talk. I had a feeling about what was going to happen. My brothers were still smiling and looking to each other. The youngest one was playing with some toys but as I expected I finally heard it:

We are getting a divorce..

I look up and see everyone in the room, they didn't see me, it was their turn to look down.. "So that was it then, was I the last drop?"

I will pick you up in a week, I love you..

The time past slowly, I was so angry with both of my parents. "What did I do wrong?" My father was even not there to say goodbye. One month past since the news of the divorce. Everything changed but yet it was still the same, until now. My parents didn't speak anymore at home, my father was always working outside, my mother was inside doing the things she always did.

"I am not wanted at home, it was all my fault. If I was not like this, they would still be together."

I am laying in my bed, everything dark around me, again. This time it was my choice to close my eyes and there were screams, more than ever, but this time it was me.. It was quiet in my head.

For my Erasmus friends

I wonder because the life is not long,
try with everybody to get along.
Hard to write and hard to see,
big dream to be completely free.
You guys, this wonderful that we are together,
that we could manage to be here no matter
as we can say hi, and keep working, smiling
as the sun goes up and gives light and shining.
We believe that we are nothing like special
and respect each other and accept as equal.
I will miss you, your kindness and party face
but remember that time goes and fill the space
with good memories and nice acts,
find a goal and dont sleep, like in cave the small bats.
Family, job, peace , nation , happiness and beliefs
stay with you forever to grow wiser buddies.

I wonder what you should do

I wonder what you should do
I wonder how much you grew

Sometimes you have to let go
But that's why I have you, my bro

I will be there for you
There's nothing I wouldn't do for you.

Nobody will hurt me this deep
Then I rather be a sleep.

Sometimes I wonder
Who is the real me?

Then I look in to the mirror.
And I wonder

Is this really me, that I see?
I could never know

If only I knew how's it going to be
If only when I try to fix things, they became better

If only I was certain of how others feel
And if only people believed what I say...

I wonder what it's to be like me?
Maybe I just want to be a bee.

I will forget all my sorrow
Just to be with you tomorrow

People (2)

I wonder what I would do
if there were no people in my life who have crossed my path,
I wonder what I would do
if there were no people in my life who made me feel happy,
I wonder what I would do
if there were no people in my life in which trust in
In which find an hand when things are going in the wrong way

I wonder what I would do
if there were no people in my life with whom I could share my secrets and confidences
I wonder what I would do
if there were no people in my life with whom I could stand beside them and join them in all the smallest sides of their life

But I have
Some of them pass through the journey of life by my side,
And I could see others just between one step and another
I'm really glad to them

They are like the sun after a lot of raining days
(And at the moment I can really say this!)
They are like the Friday after the all week working,
They are like a BIG glass of cold water after a long run

Everybody has his own life,
Everybody has his own dreams
But we are going together across the world
We are like a family

With a lot of problems sometimes, of course!

But we are still a family
Everyone is linked together
I'm feeling rich

And full of emotions
Like a rainbow shining in the sun after the rain
It is a fortune

And I wonder what I would do
if my life didn't reserve me this great fortune
I really would like to say thanks.
Thanks to Giorgia, Luca, Gaia, Fabio, Giulia, Valentina, Lia, Nicholas
I really love you!

Dear. Truth

I wonder if there is Truth,
attracting people since the oldest time
of human beings. However we try to get
closer to it, it is just getting away and away,
like we're running toward the sun. Whoever try
to figure it out, it is just making him depressed
and depressed, like struggling to get out of
a bottomless swamp. Complete hopeless is
always the consequence of the struggle.
Overwhelming uncoverability renders them
coward enough to run away to a another world.
If there is Truth, please overcome your shyness,
please come to the world, and say hello to us.
Is that too much to ask? I really want to see you.
I know you like to show us the power of belief
by being the way you are. We've been doing it since
the time when our foot touched on the planet.
Forgive me, if I'm rude, but I think you don't know
how much power and influence you can be in
possession of. You don't know how much ardent
we can be to find you. Please, take even one step
toward us, and get closer to us. You might think it is
a meaningless burden, but we have counted on you.
You have been a hope. You have been the purpose.
You have been expected. You need to be exposed.
If you are there, and if I am good enough to
understand you, please let me take a glimpse of you.
I wouldn't be disappointed even if you showed
your vulnerability to the high expectations
we've pushed on you. I wouldn't be disappointed
even if you had a total discrepancy from our creation,

and weren't good enough to play the role
as a life maker. Just let us do anything other than
to believe in you.

Be yourself, be different

I wonder what is so special about us
Yet we are still so similar.
People tend to say we are different
But is it really so?

Have you ever met someone who looked just like you?
Or someone who acted as you would, too?
What makes us so ordinary,
But unique at the same time?
Is it the look or our feelings
Or everything combined?

Are we born the same
And become different through life
Or are we born different
And tend to copy the others?

Austria
The Box

I have a box. A chest. A treasure chest.

The corners and edges of this chest are broken and dents and scratches give it an unloved appearance. But I love this chest. Actually, less the chest, but more its contents. In this chest are treasures. Treasures that have value only for me. it are small reminders of bygone days.

Broken, Old, Used.

Broken glasses, feathers, stones, shells, laces and tons of other found objects, whose value is immense for me.

All these objects, small and large, are silent witnesses of my story.

In addition to alleged waste in this chest is a T- shirt. A men's T- shirt.

When this shirt has landed in the chest, an epoch of my life comes to an end and with it the time of collecting. The chest was closed and banished to the attic.

Its content is intended to give one day my children stuff to dream.

The t-shirt is actually yellow. I hate the color yellow.

But how else could it be, I loved the former wearer of this piece of fabric. This love affair is long gone. I think less and less of the former wearer of this shirt. His image faded increasingly and I suppose that's a good thing.

Despite this, or perhaps because of it, I am a bit afraid of my treasure chest and the shirt in it. Too often, this simple piece of cloth has torn open old wounds with fangs and spread its poison in it...

Just to mention one thing: I am a simple girl. I love people and I love the love... Although I neither understand the one nor the other...

and actually I have a problem with trusting in others. I am afraid to get hurt. Again. But if I would be asked about my life dream, I would probably start taking about that old story of meeting Mr. Right, planting a tree, building a house, having children and live happily till the end of my days…

I wanted to forget my box and its contents- but to tell this story, I'll open it again. Just once.

    I kneel down in front of the chest. I open it slowly. Slowly, because I do not know how strong the wave of emotions that could arise from the crate will be and I do not want to be swept away. Not again.

    The t-shirt is on top.

    I touch it. The fabric is a little worn and you can see at first sight that it never was of particularly good quality. It's a cheap T-shirt. The seams are bad and open in some places on. My brain wants to lure me into a trap: very briefly rises the scent of the former wearer of the shirt in my nose… It does not matter. I ignore it.

    Images of the body, this t-shirt once covered come to my mind … I'll allow it.

    Just once.

    Then the future will begin.

    I promise it to myself!

    This body was beautiful for me.

    Soft, caramel-colored skin. Dark hair. Long, dark lashes. Eyes like coal.

    Eyes that knew me better than almost all other pairs of eyes that come to my mind.

    Eyes that have seen much pain and eyes that long for a stay after a long, hard travel.

    Eyes that can carry a lot of anger and eyes that are not always honest.

    Nevertheless, beautiful eyes.

    Eyes, in which I was often lost.

Eyes that could let me sink.

Eyes that made me fall. Fall on many levels - even on the level of my dignity.

Oriental - eyes. War - eyes. Fear- eyes, Fanatical eyes.

Fanatical in the performance of their duties: honoring the motherland, honoring the father, honoring Allah. Praying. 5x a day.

Eyes of a lost one. A torn one. Torn between a big love and the ultimate devotion to religion.

Eyes of one who wakes up at night crying because in the dream the bombs fall again and again and beloved persons die again and again. Are killed. Are slaughtered.

Eyes of a survivor.

The survivor is young. Too young to have a life behind him, that contains enough misery for hundreds.

The survivor is not stupid, even if he does not know much. The survivor believes everything.

The brain of the survivor was washed from an early age- without the use of fabric softener, that's for sure. Dschins lurk in his brain. And thoughts of guilt. Guilt to Allah and the family. Love to unbeliever - the largest debt of all.

As the eldest son of an old family of Taliban you should think twice about your actions. A Talib - a Koran scholar should pray and obey his fate.

A Talib should under no circumstances be together with an unbeliever- one that looks strange men in the eye, one that shows open her hair without remorse. Bitch. No, a Talib should not do that. Under no circumstances. Never. Not one minute. And certainly not weeks, months and finally years.

A Talib should make absolutely sure to love and honor.

Of course only pure being.

Pigs and infidels thus excluded.

"Should, must ... nothing than force ..." I think when I show up in reality again and t I close the box. Now it is enough.

I feel trapped.

The ropes, that are holding together this again and again glued organ that determined about my life and death, are too closely.

I would like to take them off, but I'm afraid that this poorly repaired, woody organ then disintegrates. I do not want that. The ropes remain.

Perhaps one day there might comes a Samtfinger, grind the underground and plant a new seedling.

Maybe this day is today.

I Wonder what I'd be doing now

I wonder what I'd be doing now
If I'd done things differently then
If I'd listened to all of that wisdom
If I'd put some effort in

I wonder where I would be
If I'd tried a little bit more
If I'd been brave enough to risk it
If I'd forced my way through the door

I wonder what I'd have become
If I'd taken a different road
If I'd pushed a little bit deeper
If I'd carried a different load

I wonder what I'd have achieved
If I'd gotten myself a degree
If I'd had a great job, if I'd travelled the world
If people had seen me succeed

But if all of that had happened I might never have met
You
And that would be so bad
I'd be standing in the darkness and feeling like I didn't have a
Clue
And I would feel so mad
I'd be trying to find my way, but never reaching where I'd want to
Be
Because You wouldn't be here
But You are here, I know You're right here, deep inside of
Me
And it makes me feel

Happy
I know You're always here
With me

You'll never leave me nor
Forsake me
I know You'll always be here

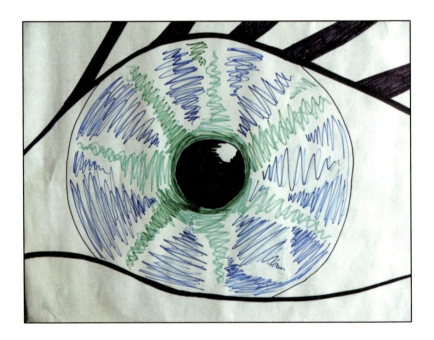

Life poem

I wonder how my life is
why some people weren't there
and how it all came to this
thank you to those who care

Some nests are emptier than others
no sisters or brothers

But people will fill up that space
mother, grandparents and friends
they are in that special place
a little part will always be theirs

They will help you when you're sad
And calm you when you're mad

And when change will come
you grab your chance
don't want it to be gone
it won't take a second glance

When important people come to your story
You never again have to worry

The puzzle of your heart
found its missing piece
It's a beautiful art
living in love and peace

Austria
How I met my boyfriend!

Dear diary

Now I'm going to tell you a story about how I met my boyfriend. Although I'm not kind of a romantic person, I think this is a romantic story.

It was in the beginning of 2009. During this time of my life that Friday evening was a normal weekend-party-night. We started the party at my place, sitting together with a couple of wine bottles with the goal to dance all night long in one of our favorite party locations. This location is not a noble disco – definitely not! In earlier times it used to be a slaughterhouse, now it's a cool concert venue, especially you can find there fine rock and punk tunes.

Already drunk we were standing in a long queue in front of the entrance. From the outside we were able to hear the music and started to dance. Step by step we danced ourselves closer to the entrance. Inside we ran into the dancing hall und just moved our bodies uncontrollably. It seemed like several vortexes were crashing into the dancing hall. Only two other guys were on the dance floor, they danced crazy as we moved. One of the two guys was a redhead, I didn't expect more than just dancing, especially because redheads weren't the type of my desires. It took some time for us to create a circle, but finally we all danced together. Sometimes we exchanged glances, we were laughing a lot and did some Pogo moves. One of the next songs the DJ played was "Dance with somebody" from Mando Diao. It was one of my favorite songs at this time. We looked each other deeply into the eyes, and I saw he loved the song as much as me. From one moment to the other we were kissing. I remember it was a really weird feeling. We kissed, then I stopped and ran away, actually I didn´t want to kiss. Then he found me again and we were kissing again. The time went by really fast, but I didn`t feel it that way. Finally I didn't tell him my telephone number, when he was asking. I just told him that my name is Sonja, I'm studying education science at the university of Vienna and if a common future is fated, he will find me. Actually I thought it's impossible to find me. But already on the next day, I had a message in my studivz-mailbox (the former Facebook in Austria), from a guy I hardly remembered, but despite with a feeling I spent a great time with. I know now that it was a really hard work to find me, there were about 400 other Sonjas on this social media platform and he took a look at every single profile.

It was worth it, because this was the start of a new lifetime for both of us and the story of how I met my boyfriend.

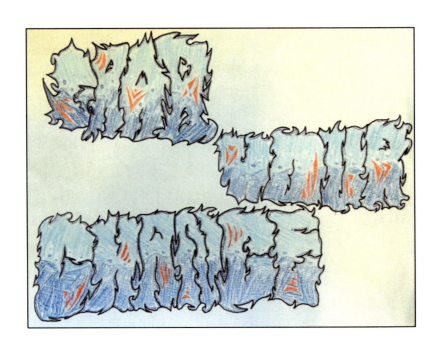

I wonder why

Is love something that can happen on first sight?
I think that it's possible
You just meet someone on purpose
because it has to be like this
Fate decides what will happen in life
And so you can become man and wife

I wonder why people fall in love with each other
Maybe it is because love is the most important thing in life

The first time we met
we didn't know what future would bring us
First we became normal friends
But after a while I felt in love
He didn't realize it in the beginning
But after some time he send me the words
"love is everywhere"

I still wonder why we fell in love
Is it because I feel safe and beloved?
We are like best friends
Who are there for each other

I can be myself with this person
He loves me the way I am
He is always there to support me in hard times
That's why I could come here
And why we will survive this

I wonder why I'm more than in love with the best person in the world!

Belgium
Life is too short!

My life started on the 28th of September in 1992. On that day, I've met my grandmother for the first time. I don't know what her reaction was when she saw me for the first time but I know she loved me from the first moment. She cared for me and my sister with her whole heart from little children to young adults. Every day after school we went to her to eat and play until my parents came to pick us up. When I was 4 years old my grandfather died and my grandmother had a complete breakdown. She was crying a lot also when we, the really little children, were there. It changed her life but we were still there and she always took care of us even if she was feeling bad or sad. She was a strong woman and she always tried to make us happy but actually she was deeply unhappy.

    A few years later she became weak in health. She never wanted to go to the doctor when she had a problem so when she was feeling ill her children had to oblige her to go to the doctor. Everyone was very close to each other at that moment and we supported each other but I had the feeling that my close family (parents) was more involved with the whole situation because her son and daughter lived further away than us. At that moment cancer was diagnosed. Before we got the diagnosis we actually knew that there was something wrong so we were not so shocked when we heard it but it was hard to handle with the thoughts. They started the therapy against the cancer very soon. The doctors gave us a lot of hope that she would survive this but from the beginning we actually knew that it was hopeless. She was very thin and couldn't eat anymore so she was really weak during the therapy. They had to stop the chemo because it was too much for her body. Than fear overtook me because I knew that she would die very soon. The last months were traveling between home and hospital. She was able to live at home but it was a great burden on my family's shoulders. On the 2nd of October 2009 the nurse who helped her at home called my mother. She didn't open the door because she had fallen on the floor that night and couldn't get up alone. It happened early in the morning before I had to go to school. I actually didn't know what was happening because my mother just left the house to go to her mother. When I was at school she sent me a message to say that they were in the hospital to take care of her. That day we knew that the end was very near. The last day that I saw her, she was sleeping. The atmosphere in the hospital was very tense and disagreeable. Our thoughts were correct. She died around 7 o'clock in the evening of 3 October 2009. I will never forget that day. I was with friends in a café when my father called me to say that she had died earlier this evening. My friends were close to me to take care of me and support me at that moment but all I wanted was to be alone. The week between her death and the funeral was the hardest week of my life. Everyone had to arrange the funeral in such a short time. We had to choose texts, music… But on the day of the funeral I had time to say goodbye in my own way. I've seen her for the last time wicht I think was terrible for me but it helped me to say goodbye. From then on it went better every day but I miss her always more and more because there are things that are happening in my life that I would like to share with her.

    She was actually my second mother, the person I could talk with, laugh with, and feel comfortable with. She was my friend and the person who taught me a lot about life and how to live a good life. The day she died will remain in my memory forever. I also want to say sorry for the times that we were angry about her and left her alone in her house and in the hospital. But it was good for her and for us. We had a very good time together and I know she was and would be so proud to be our grandmother, our 'Mami'!

I wonder how the sun can shine

I wonder…
…how the sun can shine while it's raining.
When we don't see clouds
We are uncomplaining
I wonder…
…that birds always stay at one place
While they can fly around the world.
And they always have the same pace.
I wonder
…how we can dream in the night.
But the day after,
We know that it wasn't right.
I wonder…
..how you can smile while you're sad.
That people can be happy
And the other time can be mad.
I wonder…
…how people can be enemies
And friends at one time
For each other totally estrange.
I wonder…
…why we have one chance to live
And make your life beautiful
So … be creative.

Austria
A bit of chocolate cream

With great pleasure I dug the spoon into the glass of Nutella. I swirled the chocolate around it and slowly lifted the spoon out of the glass and looked at the chocolate cream which stuck on it. I took a bite and closed my eyes. The cream melted on my tongue and I felt an explosion of happiness and freedom.

When I was younger my parents, my sister and me always went to Italy with my grandfather's caravan. After we had parked the vehicle on the camp ground, we headed for the supermarket. My mum made sure that we bought a lot of fresh fruits and vegetables, my dad wanted to have some sausages, my sister needed orange juice and I begged them to buy a glass of Nutella. Mum would say, "But only a small one. You have to be economical and not eat everything on the first day." Now my holidays could start! For breakfast I had white bread with lots of chocolate cream. After all the bread had gone, I took a spoon and kept on eating the cream.

I remember when I stayed at a hotel in Prague, where we could choose from a big breakfast buffet, and I decided to eat only bread with Nutella. My grandmother was not so happy about my choice and tried to convince me that I needed something healthy as well.

At home I never have Nutella. I really try to eat healthy and at mornings it is very important for me to have my bread with cheese, which keeps me going all day. But when I am in another country I long for a breakfast alternative. That is one thing I really look forward to.

I can compare my life to bread with cheese. In my opinion I am leading a normal life. Nobody's life can be more normal than mine. I have never experienced something really bad and I don't live an excessively exciting life. I guess my life is kind of boring, but boring in a good way.

When I am at home I often dream about travelling and seeing a lot of different places on this great world. So I went to Taiwan to experience life in a big city. I stayed three weeks in California to learn what it means for a teenage girl to attend high school in the USA. Last summer I was an au pair in Canada and had not only the possibility to spend time with a wonderful family but also almost met a black bear in the forest. Once I rode a camel close to Ayers Rock in Australia. You might be wondering, why on earth there are camels in the desert of Australia. You might ask yourself if there aren't supposed to be kangaroos. Yeah, if I had chosen to write about this I would have told you more about this really interesting topic, but I am sorry, you have to find it out on your own. If I made you curious now, I am sure you can look it up on the Internet and solve this mystery.

For my family it is not so easy to understand and accept my desire for travelling. They think I don't like them or my home country very much. But that is not true. I really love Austria, although the politicians, TV series and school can sometimes be a bit annoying. It is a wonderful country and I see myself as very happy to be born in such a peaceful country. I am sure that I have the best family who you could ever have wished for. No matter what I am doing I know that their love for me is unconditional. I am so grateful for this love and I am really sorry if I upset them with not always wanting bread with cheese.

But sometimes you need a diversion in your diet and then you need chocolate cream.

I finished the last bite and licked the remaining chocolate from the spoon and closed the glass.

As I happily leaned back and looked into the warm Danish sun, my neighbor knocked on my door and asked, "Please, can I borrow your glass of Nutella?"

Inside

I wonder
How's big a world?
And where is my place in it?
Where are my friends?
Where is my love?
I wonder…try to find it.
My dreams come true I am alone
And happiness is here
But nobody is near me
To share all these feelings.

In front of me
There is a world.
Which I try to discover
Inside me a lot of hurts
Which I try to recover
My past is not behind me
But not inside me either
It's very difficult to live
With many strange aliens

And only thing I have with me –
It is my open heart.
And thank you God
I have my mum, my lovely mum inside.
My family is near me
And every time is here.
And I believe, I want, I wish
This to exist for years.
And their love, support, respect
Will help me to give up my fears.

I wonder how's big the world
And every day and every night
I'm asking God
To ease my frights
To help me longer fight.

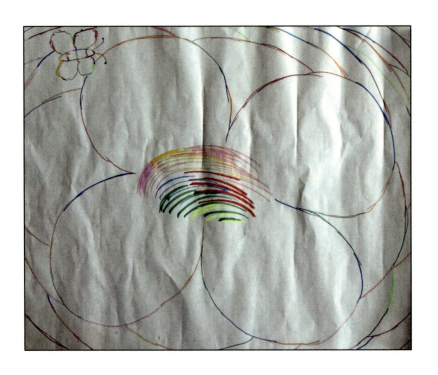

Tree

I wonder about the wonder tree
Do you know him, have you ever seen him?
He will astonish you, when you see
He's not like any other tree.
An ancient giant, planted as a small seed
Will transform into one of the most glorious things you'll ever meet.
Protected by a soft colourful foliage, you can think about
What it would be like to have your head up in a cloud.
Squirrels running energetically over his arms
A home for everyone, he's a lucky charm.
He's like a human with water running through his veins
It's so sad that he's attached to his chains.
This chains are rooted, deep within the earth
Where this age-old tree found birth.
The warm sun is shining through the leaves
But when they catch the light, they're actual thieves.
A tree is not a death thing you can claim.
Don't harm him for wood you want to obtain.
In the forest they all stand together with different identities
But are they actual friends or enemies?
One only can grow there where he finds light,
So don't bring shadow over him, but shine bright.
His green, yellow, brown or red leaves are waving in the wind
But when they fall down, there only remains bared skin.
Blossoms and buds will appear
And the sky again will be clear.
This immemorial tree will last till 'who knows when'
And we will think about him, now and then.

I wonder how it is to be another person

I wonder how it is to be another person
To see the life from a different view
I don't know if I would get the clue
But I'm sure I would choose to be you.

I would like to know what it is for you
To be happy, to laugh and to see the true
Would it be the same like me?
What would love mean to you?

For me it is not always clear
What to think from what I hear
How to act in my own life
But would I still in yours survive?

I wonder how you feel
What your thoughts are when you're still
Do you see the world like me?
Or what can you see?

Does it has to be like this
Or is it just the way it is?
When cannot do
A change between me and you

I would like to know you more
Maybe it would change the way it was before
But I think it has to be
Something special between you and me

Belgien
Orion

If the stars could speak that day, even whisper or mumble a few stammering fragments of words, they would have told me about the whimsicality, the passage of regards, glances and peeks. I couldn't tell if it were them, leading me to this place and time, yet my thoughts were out there with them for countless heartbeats whilst I was walking through the night. If any, which eyes would see me that night and bring me home in a world that was immeasurable and vast? Eyes, they are everything I see and feel. Thoughts of others, creeping upon me as if it were tendrils looking for a place in the sun where they could linger and rest, be given solace and illumination.

But not this couple of beady eyes was gazing upon me with expectations and impressions, for the latter always fall upon me like dew that covers a blossom in the early sunlight. These eyes were unlike all the others that sometimes withdraw me from the crowdiness, into my dreams and anxiety. They rested upon me and wanted nothing, not even a convenient 'hello', not a thimble of fluency and congeniality. They stood there and watched, like the sun through a window without burning me up inside. They were sweet and kind, fetterless and secure. They followed me from this night on and could not seem to find their way back home. They themselves were blindsided and wandering. Very sudden and unexpectadly, they were walking in and out of my thoughts and had a look into my world. What did they expect there to be, alongside the bits of curiosity and marvel which overwhelm me every day? Very carefully they left their words unspoken, but filled me with thousands of stuttered letters, shyness, puzzlement and loveliness.

They led me through narrow alleys and overlooked the riverside, next to me on little benches where I let my legs dangle above the water. The silence went on for hours and hours each night and took me to a place I had never been before. There, I was built up with the softness of a feather and the patience of a skillful painter, waiting for the colours to merge into the right palette. The eyes never left my side and started painting a face of their own. This was the face of tenderness, reliance and connectedness. It was all I wanted to see, even in times when it became blurred or unreachable. It took time to understand the different curves and lines that had been marked into it, but these shapes were all I wanted to fit my face into. And I tried, I still try every day. It became the face I look upon into the mirror, since the years have taught how our carves correspond. Our ways go together and this is all I ever knew, since the day its eyes caught me with their blue tinted caress.

We meet now every day, under the constellation of stars that appears to us in the same way, wherever we are. We are connected in a silence that only we can understand. It is the quietness that has always comforted us and carried us miles away into the night. Without saying a word, I comprehend every touch, every look and every sound. Through His eyes I feel his heart beating, strongly and aloud. He is not silent at all, He equals the sound of a million fluttering butterflies waiting for the right moment to come about in spring.

Up in the Air

I wonder if you get what I say
when I say "now" do I mean this day?
Do you live, do you feel,
can you breathe the air?
Do you live now and is your life fair?

Let's say "No!"
Let's say there's just rubbish in your way
So let's waste our time on what other people say!
Our world is cruel
You have to fight every single day
You're under pressure
You can't break out
You're suck in a system
of which the system is proud!

So let's waste our time
on thinking about what other people think of us
Let's go on a small trip in a small bus
Let's drive to the ocean right into the sea
Let's drown together
'cause together we're free

We'll meet on the other side of the Jordan
where time disappeared
All our rubbish has been recycled
and nothing is weird

I wonder if you get what I say
when I say "now" do I mean today?
Do you live, do you feel,

can you breathe the air?
Do you live right now and is your life fair?

Let's say "NO!"
But just don't care
Let's say "Shit, I don't throw myself away!"
What if you die
and you've wasted your time
What if there's no heaven
would that also be fine?

Then we can't meet nowhere
Nowhere isn't there
We can't meet on the other side
so choose: you want to live or to hide?
You can choose because you exist
You exist right now
You can decide
even if there's no how

You can open this door
You can step outside
explore this world
'cause you are your own guide

I'm not you
You can't live my life
I won't live yours
That's what I decide

And when I'm old
I want to sit on a chair
I want to tell my stories
because my stories have been there

And when I die
At old age or not
When I die
And it's my last spot
I won't wonder if I've wasted my time
'cause I've lived
Every day, every hour, every second
It was me, my life, it was mine

So I wonder if you get what I say
when I say "now" do I mean this day?
Do you live, do you feel,
can you breathe this air?
Do you get these words?
Do you get what's out there?

Not only a Dream

It happened in the summer. Mama was watching TV and saw a program about an interesting and famous guy. She told me that this man "special for me"; intelligent, beautiful and popular. He is a singer and writer. I smiled because I knew that it was only a dream... After a while I was traveling on the sea. Mama insisted that I found him on Facebook and wrote to him. I did just that. I wrote him the following.... "Good day N, I did not want to write you but obedience to my parents is very important for me. If you were interested, you can answer me (and I described my hobbies in brief). Soon after he replied. We started to talk but not much. I once sent him a photo of the church that was next to the sea. He was surprised and asked me what I did in this city. I replied that I had travelled there. That was a coincidence, he said, for after 2 days would will be in this town, because he has a cottage there.

On the third day we met. It was an amazing meeting, we sunbathed and swam and talked. Then we went to the market, he showed me the city. A guy like Guy, I thought. But it was time to say goodbye, he said to me "with God". And these words, like sediment remained in my heart.

Two months have passed since then and he came to my town for a concert. Now we meet more often.

Students' evaluation remarks on the process of writing this book

- These classes were a nice experience as we all had a chance to try ourselves as writers and poets. It took a lot of creativity from us
- The Line Game is indeed a really nice thing!
    - I liked the Line Game, which helped us to understand our mates situation, to learn something from them
    - Inspiring!
    - Some questions were too personal
    - I admit it can be very uncomfortable, but avoiding the difficult things makes people scared – facing the darkness makes us stronger and better people
- This is a great way to be more confident about yourself and not to be ashamed of your past
    - You start to realize that everybody has been through stuff
    - I started to be more open after I saw others to be so
    - I don't think this course will stop me (or anyone else) from feeling shame
- It is sometimes really hard to go in front of the class and be "vulnerable" for everyone…
    - I think it made many people uncomfortable in the beginning
- This is too heavy (mentally)!
    - Heavy yes, but it is your own decision to make it 'too' heavy
    - It was heavy sometimes, but I agree it can help you to think about stuff
    - It helped me to make some things
- We sometimes revealed too personal things
    - I agree because sometimes it was very hard to show others our past

- - This is a group of 'strangers'. You don't know everybody that well
  - Disagree. You tell as much as you want
  - We all told stories but we did not get to the real content with each other and the teacher. In this way the content seemed unimportant
- I didn't like it that we only could write one story. I would have likes to write more stories – more like a diary
- I learned how to put feelings into words
- The lessons taught me to be another person – deal with my problems
- I enjoyed having the opportunity to write in two different genres
  - Poems are good
  - It was surprising but nice
- Writing in English was difficult
  - True, but it increases our language skills
  - And it is in the spirit of the original Freedom Writers
  - Writing about feelings is hard, but in a foreign language even harder!
- Sometimes it was embarrassing to talk about myself!
- You gave us the impression the story had to be something serious. By watching the movie a lot of stories became a bit depressed and serious…
- Contradiction: <u>Freedom Writer</u>, but for us it was a forced 'frredom' – we had to write!
- I like the fact that we wrote a book!
  - For some people the only opportunity to do it